P9-BIB-075

Basel in the Sixteenth Century

Aspects of the City Republic before, during, and after the Reformation

HANS R. GUGGISBERG

CENTER FOR REFORMATION RESEARCH
ST. LOUIS, MISSOURI

Basel in the
Sixteenth Century

Library of Congress Cataloging in Publication Data

Guggisberg, Hans R. (Hans Rudolf), 1930-
   Basel in the sixteenth century.

   Includes bibliographical references and index.
   1. Reformation--Switzerland--Basel--Addresses, essays,
lectures. 2. Basel (Switzerland)--Church history--
Addresses, essays, lectures. 3. Basel (Switzerland)--
History--Addresses, essays, lectures. 4. Humanism--
History--Addresses, essays, lectures. I. Center for
Reformation Research. II. Title.
BR410.G83 1982   274.94'3   82-22066
ISBN 0-910345-00-7

Contents

Preface

The purpose of this little book is to describe and discuss some aspects of the history of Basel in the sixteenth century. Although this history has never before been told in the English language, the reader should not expect a comprehensive narrative. What he will receive is no more than a first orientation—an orientation, however, which will hopefully entice him to turn to more voluminous secondary works and eventually to the sources themselves.

I shall confine myself to a selection of facts and problems, but I hope to succeed in showing that most of them are of more than only local relevance. In the first chapter I shall discuss the constitutional, political, and socio-economic situation of the Basel city republic at the end of the Middle Ages as well as the rise of humanism in the early decades of the sixteenth century. The second chapter will deal with the Reformation and quite particularly with the relationship between the religious renewal and the already existing political and social tensions. In the third chapter I shall try to draw a portrait of the "Basilea reformata" in the post-Reformation era, and in the fourth and concluding chapter I shall discuss the case of an opponent of the Reformed establishment whose intellectual achievement is considered to be of general consequence for the history of early modern Europe by 20th century historians: I shall deal with Sebastian Castellio and the origins of the debate on religious toleration.

One basic fact must be mentioned at the outset: Twice during the sixteenth century Basel was a cultural center of more than local or regional importance, first at the time of Erasmus of Rotterdam's residence before 1529 and then again from about 1550 through the early 1580s. During both periods Basel attracted a great many visitors from all over Europe and also sent a considerable number of intellectual impulses to other cities and countries. It seems appropriate to describe Basel as a focal point of European culture in the late Renaissance period. But let us not exaggerate: the city republic on the upper Rhine was only one among many such focal points and perhaps not even one of very great importance. In saying this I am fol-

lowing the judgment of the great Polish historian Stanisław Kot
who, before and during World War II, wrote a number of substan-
tial studies on the intellectual relations between Poland and Western
Europe in the sixteenth century. In an article on Poles in Basel during the reign of Sigismund August (1548–1572), which he published
in 1942, Kot emphasized the fact that Basel had provided considerable intellectual stimulation to Polish scholars and aristocrats. But in
the introductory paragraph he very clearly stated: "Basel was neither Rome nor Wittenberg, neither Geneva nor Paris."[1] With these
words Kot did not minimize the importance of Basel, but he set it
apart quite distinctly from that of the European capitals of the sixteenth century. His differentiation still seems fair and valid today. It
will be kept in mind throughout our deliberations.

The following four chapters were originally devised and written
as lectures. They were presented at Smith College in 1978 (chapter
IV) and during the fall semester of 1980 (chapters I–III) when I
served as Kennedy Guest Professor. Parts of chapter III were also
read to the 1980 meeting of the Sixteenth Century Studies Confer-
ence in St. Louis. For publication all four lectures were revised,
partly rewritten, and annotated.[2]

The publication of this book was made possible by the generosity
of the Center for Reformation Research in St. Louis. I particularly
wish to thank William S. Maltby, the Executive Director of the Center, for his initiative and support. For valuable advice and encour-
agement I am indebted to Miriam Usher Chrisman (University of
Massachusetts, Amherst). My friends and colleagues at Smith College made my visit to their delightful grove of academe a very in-
structive and rewarding experience. My thanks go to them all,
notably to Nelly S. Hoyt and Joachim Stieber.

Basel, April 1982   H.R.G.

Chapter I

The Late Medieval City and the Rise of Humanism

As the title indicates, this chapter will consist of two parts. In the first part, which is designed to provide a background to our general theme, I shall try to give an outline of the political and constitutional structure of the Basel city republic in the late fifteenth and early sixteenth centuries. It will be necessary to point to a few facts of its earlier history. Particular attention will be paid to its relationship with the Swiss Confederation at around 1500. A few remarks will be devoted to the ecclesiastical institutions and to the early history of the University of Basel. The second part will treat the first flowering of humanism. In this context I shall discuss the reasons why Basel could become a center of humanist learning; after this I shall try to describe some characteristic aspects of the Basel humanist movement and then conclude with a description of the role of Erasmus of Rotterdam within that movement.

Situated at the intersection of several trade routes, Basel at the beginning of the sixteenth century was a commercial center of more than only regional significance. It had a population of approximately 10,000. Together with Geneva it ranked first among the cities of the territory of modern Switzerland. Among the cities of the German Empire, however, Basel belonged to the medium category. It was only half as large as Strasbourg or Nuremberg.[1] As a free imperial city, Basel stood in the same category with other episcopal and archipiscopal sees such as Regensburg, Strasbourg, Worms, Speyer, Mainz, and Cologne.[2] All through the medieval centuries the city council of Basel had conducted a continuous and often successful struggle to free the urban republic from the domination of the bishop. An important milestone on this road toward political independence had been reached in 1386. In that year King Wenceslas had issued the so-called Prague Charter which transferred the imperial stewardship to the city council. At the same time the city was able to purchase the rights over "Kleinbasel" (the section north of the Rhine) from the sons of Duke Leopold III of Austria who had lost his life in the battle of Sempach. Further steps toward political consolidation were taken before 1400 as well as in the late fifteenth and early sixteenth centuries. Some of these steps will be mentioned later on.

The year 1501 brought a real turning point in the history of Basel. In that year Basel became a full member of the Swiss Confederation. Since then the city republic on the Rhine has been part of Switzerland, but within the Confederation Basel has often maintained a somewhat special position. More than once it was in danger of isolating itself and one such instance will be discussed later on,[3] but its membership in the Confederation has never again been called into question. One of the crucial paragraphs of the treaty of 1501 stated that in case of conflict between other members of the League Basel should not take sides but act as a mediator.[4] The city republic has always taken this obligation very seriously. It has fulfilled its duty on several occasions, although not always with success. The willingness to mediate and the tendency to find pragmatic solutions in a spirit of moderation have become characteristic elements of the interior political life of the city of Basel and also of its role in the political affairs of Switzerland.[5]

Looking back upon the political situation of Basel and the Swiss League in the late fifteenth century, we cannot overlook the fact that both sides were interested in establishing a union. The Swiss wanted the wealthy commercial town in their Confederation mainly for financial and economic reasons, Basel's political leaders saw that the city could not thrive as an independent republic between the Empire, France, and Switzerland. How dangerous the situation could become had been very obvious during the so-called "Swabian War" of 1499 in which Emperor Maximilian I had unsuccessfully tried to force the Swiss into a closer association with the Empire. By joining the Confederation, Basel obviously had to sacrifice some of its dignity as an imperial estate. From the new allies the council obtained formal assurance of perpetual protection against any possible aggressor.[6] This did not mean very much, however. Basel remained an outpost on the northern periphery of the Confederation. Aggression from the North and Northeast would always hit it before it affected the other members of the League. Another point is even more important: The city republic had to re-orient itself not only politically but also economically. Up to 1501 its natural "Hinterland" had been the Alsace in the North and Northwest; now it was the territory of the Swiss Confederation to the South. A considerable portion of the Alsace was part of the Basel diocese, and many monasteries in the city as well as the cathedral chapter owned property there. Many noble Alsatian families had settled or acquired houses in Basel during the Middle Ages. Alsatian scholars and students lived here in considerable numbers since the foundation of the University and the rise of the bookprinting industry. The manifold relations between Basel and the Alsace were, of course, not severed at once. They continued to exist throughout the Reformation period, but afterwards they gradually lost their former intensity.[7] Immediately to the South and Southeast of the city lay its own rural territory. The "Landschaft" was an agglomeration of rural dominions which had been acquired in the course of the Middle Ages. It was about as large as the actual canton Baselland.

The bishops had created the city; they had been responsible for its growth. In 1080 one of them built the first city walls. Another had constructed the first bridge across the Rhine in 1225. The bishops had also established the guilds, the oldest charter ("zunftbrief") dating from 1226. A city council was created in 1212. Its very limited powers and the bishops' authority over its composition were formally defined for the first time in the episcopal constitution ("Handveste") of 1263, but until the early decades of the fourteenth century the practically absolute power of the bishops as overlords ("Stadtherren") remained largely uncontested. When opposition began it was at first carried on by the patricians, that is, by the aristocrats who stood in the service of the bishops, and by the wealthy merchants. Later and particularly in the fifteenth century the guilds became more and more aggressive in their struggle for political and economic independence.

At the beginning of the sixteenth century the citizenry had become very self-conscious, and after joining the Swiss Confederation it felt strong enough to deprive the episcopal overlord of all his authority. In 1521 the city council decided that nobody was allowed henceforth to take an oath before the bishop and that the bishop was excluded from exerting any influence whatsoever upon the election of the city government. That was the final breach. The bishop at that moment was too weak financially and politically to do anything to prevent this humiliation, but the conflict was far from over.[8]

When Basel had become a member of the Swiss Confederation, the immediate advantages were not obvious. Later-on, however, the move was to prove salutary. Unlike the imperial cities of Strasbourg and Constance, Basel never had to suffer under the Interim of 1548, and it was never incorporated into a monarchical state.

As I have just mentioned, the guilds had begun to play a crucial role in Basel's political life long before the Reformation. There were fifteen of them. The noble families had lost their influence in the course of the fifteenth century, and shortly after 1500 also the great merchants of the "Hohe Stube" were deprived of their political power. A new urban elite or ruling class emerged. It consisted of the leading members of the four "Herrenzünfte" (gentlemen's guilds). These guilds were called "Schlüssel" (Keys: tradesmen), "Hausgenossen" (House fellows: bankers and money changers), "Weinleute" (Wine people: wine merchants), and "Saffran" (Saffron: shopkeepers, various textile manufacturers, stationers, and bookprinters). Below them came the eleven "Handwerkerzünfte" (craft and artisans' guilds) who generally tended to be more radical in their political demands than the "Herrenzünfte."[9] From the craft guilds an increasing number of energetic and aggressive politicians began to emerge. These men were opposed not only to the bishop and to the great merchants of the "Hohe Stube" but also to the tradesmen and smaller merchants of the gentlemen's guilds. The leaders of the craft guilds were to reach the peak of their influence in the years immediately preceding the breakthrough of the Reformation. This very important fact will be discussed later.[10]

Since 1521 the city government consisted almost entirely of the delegates from the guilds. At the top of the hierarchy stood the so-called "Häupter" (heads), i.e. the "Bürgermeister" (mayor) and the "Oberzunftmeister" (superior guild master). Into the Little Council each guild delegated its guild master and one "Ratsherr"(alderman). This group always sat together with the "Häupter," and it was in these joint meetings ("Rat und Häupter") that all the important legislative, executive, and juridical decisions were taken. The Great Council consisted of six delegates from each guild (the so-called "Sechser"), the chief justices of the two city courts, four delegates from each of the three corporations of Kleinbasel, and all members of the Little Council. Within each guild the "Sechser" also constituted the executive committee or "Zunftvorstand." The main function of the Great Council was the confirmation of the Little Council's decisions. The Great Council discussed all the important matters laid before it by the Little Council, but it did not exert any real power except very briefly during the Reformation crisis. It did not convene regularly, and its meetings were usually held upon invitation by the Little Council. The posts of the "Häupter" and all the seats in the Little and Great Council were doubly filled. The incumbents functioned alternately for one year. A new council member could take office only after the death, discharge, or voluntary resignation of an old one. Membership in the councils was in principle for life. If all posts were filled—which was almost never the case— the total number of members in the new and old (functioning and non-functioning) councils rose to well over 250. The governing group, i.e. the "Rat and Häupter," consisted of sixty-four men. The day-to-day administrative work was done in a great number of committees which mainly consisted of members of the Little Council. If we want to determine the influence of one particular council member we always have to find out in which committee he served and for how long.[11]

The system of government as it existed in Basel after 1521 was not basically different from that of other Swiss towns like Zürich, Bern, or Geneva. The numerical size of the ruling elite in relation to that of the total population was roughly the same everywhere. The oligarchic structure of the governing bodies, the absence of free elections, and the general lack of regular rotation in office can also be observed in all of these other towns. It can be said, for example, that the Basel system was somewhat less exclusive than that of Bern. Its main characteristic was the dominant influence of the guilds. Their political weight was more significant than almost anywhere else. The Basel government is adequately described as a guild government or "Zunftregiment."

Like every other medieval city Basel was the home of a number of ecclesiastical institutions. In addition to the cathedral chapter there were two collegiate chapters, five major monasteries for men, and four nunneries. Smaller foundations included two knights' houses and a number of welfare institutions such as almshouses and hospitals. On the eve of the Reformation most of the monasteries had few inmates. We know for instance that in 1525 there were eight canons in the collegiate chapter of St. Leonhard, four to five monks in the Carthusian monastery, and not more than one or two in the Benedictine (Cluniacensian) monastery of St. Alban's. The Franciscan and Dominican monasteries and the women's convents were somewhat larger, the number of their inmates varying between twenty and forty. The only institution of respectable size was the cathedral chapter. In 1525 it still consisted of thirteen canons and seventy-two chaplains who served in various functions. At the same time the collegiate chapter of St. Peter had nine canons and thirty-one chaplains. Other chaplains worked in the parishes and in the hospitals. Although it cannot be denied that during the 1520s the Basel monasteries were in decay, it has been estimated that the total number of clerical persons living in the city at that time amounted to approximately four hundred, or four to five percent of the entire population.[12]

This bleak picture should not, however, create the impression that the ecclesiastical institutions of Basel had been without significance for the cultural development of the late-medieval city. If Basel became an important center of intellectual life and scholarship in the early sixteenth century, it is at least partly due to some impulses and activities which emanated from the ecclesiastical institutions. The episcopal court and the major monasteries encouraged scholarly and artistic work in many respects. We know little about the cathedral school and the monastery schools, but we know that in the later fifteenth century both the cathedral chapter and some of the monasteries employed many copyists of manuscripts, calligraphers, miniaturists, goldsmiths, painters, glass-painters, sculptors, and architects. Several monasteries possessed sizable libraries. The most famous collection of manuscripts and early printed books was that of the Dominicans. Its several hundred items had been brought together during a long period of time. The most valuable donation had come from Cardinal John Stojkovic of Ragusa who had attended the council of Basel as one of its principal theologians and representatives in its dealings with the Hussites and with the church of Constantinople. The Carthusian monastery, founded in 1401, became an important center of manuscript copying in the middle of the fifteenth century, at a time when monastic "scriptoria" had largely ceased to exist elsewhere. Like the Dominican library that of the Carthusians was very rich in illuminated manuscripts. In both collections the theological and religious works were naturally prominent, but they also contained philosophical, juridical and historiographical writings in considerable numbers. In their many-sidedness these libraries testified impressively to the wide variety of interests among prehumanist monastic scholars who were not only avid readers but also ardent collectors of beautiful books. While most of the other monastery libraries have not been preserved, the collections of the Dominicans and Carthusians have come down to us in their entirety, or at least without too many losses. They were integrated into the University library after the Reformation.[13]

When the propaganda of the religious renewal began to be heard in the Basel churches and the first editions of Luther's writings were spread among the citizens, the University was only a little more than sixty years old. It had been founded on the initiative of a number of leading citizens who still remembered the glorious time of the council when a temporary university was already in existence. The papal charter of 1459 had been signed by Pius II, who, as Enea Silvio Piccolomini, had himself attended the council as a secretary and knew Basel very well.[14] Most of the early professorships—never more than a dozen—were financed by ecclesiastical prebends, but financial support came also from the city. The school was small, and financial difficulties never ceased to oppress it. In spite of this the faculty was fairly international from the beginning and remained so until after the Reformation. Most of the teachers came from German-speaking countries, but there were always some Frenchmen and Italians among them. The number of students in the early years was approximately one or two hundred. At the end of the fifteenth century it had considerably decreased. The main reason for this decline was increasing competition from a number of other universities that had been established in Southern Germany shortly before and after 1460, e.g. Freiburg (1457) and Tübingen (1477).[15]

The significance of the University of Basel in the late fifteenth and early sixteenth centuries should not be overestimated. Although it was not left untouched by humanist concepts of learning, it remained an essentially conservative stronghold of medieval intellectual traditions. If Basel became a center of humanist culture, it was not because of the University but because of the bookprinters.

The printing industry established itself in Basel in the 1460s, i.e. shortly after the foundation of the University. The coincidence is significant: both academic instruction (however modest in scope) and the production of books contributed to the intensification of the city's intellectual life. Various factors had made it possible for the "black art" to come to Basel so early. First of all, the printers found the necessary raw materials here. Paper had been manufactured since 1435. The Basel paper-mills were not the oldest in Switzerland, but they were soundly financed and had survived the critical periods of their early existence.[16] In Basel there also lived a number of goldsmiths and other artisans who were able and adequately equipped for type cutting and bookbinding. Painters and graphic artists who could embellish the books were easily found. The University was able to provide academically trained editors and correctors who could make a living in the service of the printers. In addition to this the existence of various commercial facilities must not be overlooked. The Basel merchants of the fifteenth century had many business contacts abroad. Capital was available, and the shipment of paper and books to other Rhenish towns was comparatively simple and cheap. Transportation on land in other directions was more expensive but possible.[17] Thus Basel became widely known as a printing town well before the end of the fifteenth century. Between 1475 and 1490 three particularly able entrepreneurs settled in the city: Johannes Amerbach, Johannes Petri, and Johannes Froben ("die drei Hanse"). They all came from Franconia and were to found famous centers of learning and book production.[18] In 1501 when Basel became a member of the Swiss Confederation, more than seventy bookprinters had set up their shops in the city. They were generally welcomed by the authorities and never forced to organize themselves in a specific corporation of their trade. The bookprinting industry remained guild-free ("zunftfrei"). Bookprinting was not considered a trade like the others but rather an art or at least an artistic activity serving the *"artes liberales"* of the academic world. Not all of the printers worked independently; the more successful ones, however, soon tended to expand their activities into publishing and bookselling. Most of them employed not only learned correctors but also journeymen and apprentices. In this respect they were subject to regulations issued by the city government, but about the political activities of the printers' journeymen in Basel we know very little.[19]

There is a general consensus among modern historians that the printing industry was primarily responsible for the rise of humanism in Basel. It was a much stronger magnet than the University. The printing shops attracted the scholars because they offered opportunities for publishing. If the general program of the humanist movement consisted of the study of ancient, biblical, and early Christian texts, the elaboration of commentaries, editions, and re-editions, and the propagation of "modern" scholarly and literary writings in the classical style, the printing houses were the best places in which to do this kind of work. From here an ever-growing reading public could be reached. Discussion, inspiration, and exchange of ideas were possible. Basel was not the only city which could provide such intellectual stimulation, but it compared well with other centers of early printing such as Mainz, Antwerp, Paris, Lyons, and Venice.

The manuscripts of the monastery libraries were numerous and readily available to scholars. Among the early representatives of the Basel humanist movement we find clerics and university teachers, but also a large number of unattached scholars who took temporary employment with the major printing houses as editors and correctors. From the late fifteenth to the late sixteenth century the majority of humanist scholars who worked and published in Basel were foreigners. They came from the Alsace, from other parts of the German Empire, and later from France and Italy. Scholars who were born in Basel only gradually became prominent in the movement. The rest of Switzerland provided some colorful "humanistes de montagne," but their number was always small.[20]

The first signs of a propagation of humanist ideas had become visible during the period of the council. It was the humanism of the Italian Renaissance as represented by Enea Silvio Piccolomini. The impact must have been considerable not only among the clerics of the episcopal court and of the collegiate chapters but also among the leading citizens. Otherwise it would be difficult to explain why it was this group which after the end of the council took up the initiative toward the foundation of the University.[21] But we know very little about these early influences. Although their existence cannot be denied there is no question that the humanist movement as a movement started only after 1460, and that scholars who were not officially linked with the University played an important part in it from its beginning.

If the relative independence from educational and ecclesiastical institutions is a conspicuous characteristic of the Basel humanist movement, the second and equally important characteristic is its Christian, biblical, and ethical orientation. The Basel movement never went through a phase of paganism and it was never dominated by national or nationalistic ideas. From the beginning its main interest was directed toward the sources of Christianity. Editing the Holy Scriptures and the works of the Church fathers in their original versions was its great aim even before the arrival of Erasmus of Rotterdam. The striving for the renewal of Christian life also began long before Luther's writings became known, and we must not overlook the fact that the desire to become acquainted with the sources of Christianity was widespread not only among clerics but also among educated laymen. The chief and general concern was the expansion of knowledge and the deepening of the understanding of Christian ethics.

It is amazing that the general urge to reach these aims did not lead to disputes among the scholars in which Origen would have been played off against Tertullian, or Plato against Aristotle and the Evangelists. The Basel humanists always tended toward a harmonization of the Greek tradition of *"philosophia"* with the Hebrew-Christian heritage of *"revelatio."* This was a general tendency which can be observed throughout the sixteenth century. It may well be called the third characteristic of Basel humanism. There were always exceptions to the rule, however: some humanist scholars became defenders of the Roman Catholic church, some became leaders or staunch adherents of the Reformation, and others veered off toward spiritualistic individualism or evangelical radicalism. If one studies the biographies of these men at close range, however, one almost always finds at least some traces of the disposition toward mediation between and harmonization of opposite standpoints. Without wanting to indulge in undue speculation one might say that the main orientation of Basel politics within the Swiss Confederation had its counterpart in this general tendency of Basel humanism. Extremist positions were always shunned. A certain analogy cannot be overlooked.[22]

Our generalizing remarks about the character of Basel humanism call for some illustrations. Let me therefore now turn to the discussion of a number of basic facts and important individuals.

If we survey the period from about 1460 to 1529 we can distinguish a phase of preparation which lasted until about 1510 and preceded the actual flowering time. In this phase of preparation a few figures emerge who seem to stand for both the medieval tradition of learning and the spirit of the Renaissance. The most interesting representative of this first generation of Basel humanists was Johannes Heynlin von Stein, a native of Swabia. He lived in Basel in the mid-1460s, taught at the Faculty of Arts, and was instrumental in working out the statutes of the new University. Later-on his many-sided interests led him to Paris where he founded the first printing house and even became rector of the Sorbonne. Among his pupils were Johannes Amerbach and Johannes Reuchlin. In 1474 he returned to Basel as a preacher. With great eloquence he scourged the corruption of morals and called for a general renewal of Christian life. During a short stay in Tübingen he helped found the University of that town, but then he returned to Basel for good, preached in the cathedral and finally retired to the Carthusian monastery where he ended his days in theological study and contemplation. In the course of his vagrant life Heynlin had acquired a remarkable collection of books which he gave to the Carthusians. Most of his own works have never been printed, but several manuscript volumes of sermons, university lectures and theological tracts have been preserved and are now in the Basel University Library. Heynlin was a scholar, but also a fighter for educational and religious reform, a forerunner both of Christian humanism in the Erasmian sense and of the Reformation. The fruits of his efforts were reaped by those who came after him, and he has not yet found a biographer.[23]

The years 1510–1513 witnessed a general change in the personal structure of the Basel humanist movement. The leading men of the preparatory phase had disappeared by then. Heynlin had died in 1496. Sebastian Brant—doctor of laws, dean of the Faculty of Jurisprudence and author of the *Ship of Fools* (1494)—had gone back to Strasbourg in the spring of 1501.[24] In the first decade of the sixteenth century the printing firm of Johannes Amerbach reached its zenith. Greek and Hebrew scholars worked there on large editorial projects or corresponded with the learned master of the house; but in 1513 Amerbach died, two years after Johannes Petri and very shortly after the German Dominican Johannes Cono, who along with Reuchlin had been among the most eminent collaborators of the "Officina Amerbachiana."

The most widely respected printing firm was now that of Johannes Froben. He established himself in the house which Amerbach had used as his shop and finished some of Amerbach's publishing enterprises. Among the printers who specialized in scholarly works Froben had no serious competitor until 1519 when Andreas Cratander began to work independently.

After 1511 a number of new men appeared in the scholarly community of Basel, some of them quite young, others already in their middle age. The first was Beatus Rhenanus from Schlettstadt; after him came Ludwig Bär, Basel-born but educated as a theologian in Paris; then there appeared Heinrich Loriti Glareanus from the alpine valley of Glarus, a noted poet, musicologist, historian and a lover of jokes. A little later two biblical scholars and friends turned up, Wolfgang Fabritius Capito from Hagenau and Johannes Oecolampadius from Weinsberg in Swabia. On the periphery of the group stood several Franciscan monks including the preachers Franz Wiler and Daniel Agricola, but most prominently Conrad Pellican from Rouffach, the best Hebrew scholar after Reuchlin. Not too far away from the scholarly circle we find Christoph von Utenheim, the

learned and reform-minded Bishop of Basel. If one glances over
these names—many others could easily be added—one recognizes
the group of humanist scholars as the "Sodalitas Basiliensis" of
which there exists a very famous contemporary description:

> They all know Latin, they all know Greek, most of them know
> Hebrew too; one is an expert historian, another an experienced
> theologian; one is skilled in the mathematics, one a keen anti-
> quary, another a jurist . . . I certainly have never before had
> the luck to live in such a gifted company. And to say nothing of
> that, how open-hearted they are, how gay, how well they get
> on together! You would say they had only one soul.

These are, as everyone knows, the words of Erasmus of Rotterdam.
They appear in a letter to the Schlettstadt schoolmaster Johannes
Sapidus of February 1516. Here the Dutch humanist also describes
Basel as an *"amoenissimum museum"* (i.e. a most delightful precinct
of the Muses).[25] When Erasmus came to Basel for the first time in
August 1514 he was already world-famous. He was on his way to
Italy and wanted to stop only very briefly, but he stayed more than a
year and a half except for a trip to England in the spring of 1515.
The main attraction was the house of Froben. An edition of the
Adagia had appeared here in 1513 which Erasmus liked much better
than that of Aldus Manutius in Venice. He was also impressed by the
fact that Froben possessed the most beautiful Greek types he had
seen anywhere. Thus he decided to have the Greek New Testament
and the works of Jerome published in Basel. The preparation of
these editions kept him busy throughout his first visit.[26] Froben at
the same time also published a re-edition of the *Encomium Moriae*,
the *Institutio principis Christiani*, and the works of Seneca. Many
members of the "Sodalitas Basiliensis" collaborated in these projects.
Erasmus had found his favorite printer. He felt at ease among the
Basel scholars and quickly became the dominant figure of their community, but he did not settle down for good. From May 1516 until
November 1521 he was away again, mainly in the Netherlands and
in England. During the summer of 1518 he came back to supervise
the second edition of the New Testament. These were the years of his
highest fame. He received honors and invitations from everywhere,
but he was also increasingly criticized for wanting to remain neutral
in the religious disputes of the time. Wherever he was he worked in-
cessantly. He prepared editions of the works of Suetonius, of
Cyprianus and of other Church fathers. He revised his prefaces to

the New Testament and also started to publish his letters. In Louvain where he had helped establish the "Collegium trilingue" he was put under increasing pressure to write against Luther. When in the fall of 1521 he was called back to Basel to correct the third edition of the New Testament, he was glad to go, but the happiness of the earlier visits was only partly restored, mainly through his friendship with Froben and with Bonifacius Amerbach, the son of Johannes, who in 1525 became professor of jurisprudence.[27] Otherwise there were many problems. Erasmus had to spend a great deal of time writing against Ulrich von Hutten, Luther, and many other critics. He nevertheless continued his scholarly activity as an editor and also emended the *Colloquia*. The Sodalitas, however, was no longer what it had been. The Reformation divided spirits and created factions, and alienation from former friends and collaborators was unavoidable. When the Reformation finally won its victory in 1529, Erasmus left for Freiburg i.Br. Some friends left with him, others remained in the reformed city, notably Bonifacius Amerbach.[28]

If we look back upon the first flowering period of sixteenth century Basel humanism we can see quite clearly that the climax had been reached in the years preceding the consolidation of the Reformation movement, that is, from about 1515 to 1525. The "Sodalitas Basiliensis" was never a dull group, nor was its membership stable. Many of its members were repeatedly absent for extended periods of time. When they returned their news were eagerly awaited, and short-time visitors were always welcomed with pleasure. A lot of scholarly work was done, but there was also a great deal of conversation, conviviality, merriment, and gossip. There were no academic formalities, the association was and remained absolutely informal. Similar "sodalitates" existed in other towns. We think of Strasbourg, Augsburg, Nuremberg, and Vienna. None of these groups, however, had a leader and "spiritus rector" as internationally famous as Erasmus. He did not act as a ruler, but his superior competence and authority was recognized by all the other members of the "Sodalitas Basiliensis."

There are many testimonies of the self-confidence of the Basel humanists during the first two decades of the sixteenth century. They were proud of their achievements and repeatedly called their own time a "Golden Age." But the assertions of local glory and local pride which we find in the writings of the members of the "Sodalitas Basiliensis" have no national or nationalistic connotation. Identifi-

cation with the "inclyta Basilea" always means identification with
the ideals of the "studia humanitatis." If the Basel humanists expressed pride it was because Erasmus was or had been among
them.[29]

Enthusiasm for the lively intellectual atmosphere of Basel was
quite often outweighed by an outspoken sobriety when the material
conditions of scholarly life were discussed. In such instances the general tone became reserved and sometimes plaintive. The city of Basel
then no longer appeared as an international center of culture, but as
a small town in which people had to work hard to make a living.
When the less glamorous aspects of daily life in sixteenth century
Basel are mentioned we often notice assertions of affection, gratitude, and personal commitment which sound much more convincing than similar statements in eloquent panegyrics.

Let me present just one example. In December 1523 Johannes
Froben wrote a letter to Bonifacius Amerbach who at that time was
just finishing his studies of law at Avignon. The printer informed the
young jurist of a vacancy on the Faculty of Law in Basel. One of the
professors had just resigned and the Little Council had discussed the
possibility of offering the position to Amerbach. Now Froben writes:

> I cannot advise you to come because the salary is small. There
> are not many students. Most of them come from Switzerland,
> and you know well that they are in general not very talented.
> My dear Bonifacius, the decision is yours. If you consider it
> profitable, then come. If you think differently, I do not want
> to put any pressure upon you. Your sister, however, has much
> insisted that I urge you to come.[30]

Bonifacius came. He agreed to teach his not very brilliant Swiss
students in 1524 and received his doctorate from the Avignon law
school in the following year. Once in Basel, he quickly rose to prominence as a legal adviser, a humanist, and a protector of other
scholars.

Three points must be emphasized in conclusion: 1) The Basel humanists of the early sixteenth century were a relatively small intellectual elite in a medium-sized city republic. They appear to have
been only marginally involved in the social and political unrest of
the time, at least before the Reformation began to spread. Most of
them lived at a considerable distance from the common people; the
great majority of the population showed little interest in their activities. 2) The city government did not pay much attention to the

humanists either. Some were appointed to professorships at the University, others served as juridical advisers. Mostly they were left in peace. They did not often receive official honors, but on the other hand they were never asked to glorify the city publicly and officially. 3) The Reformation put an end to the first flowering of humanism in Basel, but it did not extinguish the "studia humanitatis" forever. They were to rise again after 1530 and to go through a "Renaissance" of their own which reached its climax after the middle of the century.

The Reformation: Religious Renewal in a Time of Political and Economic Tensions.

Among historians who devote themselves to the study of sixteenth century Europe the debate on the role of the cities in the Reformation has been going on for some time. In recent years it has centered mainly on the cities of Germany and Switzerland. With few but notable exceptions, French, English, and Scandinavian cities have not yet been drawn into the picture.[1]

Like the debate on the Peasants' War, that on the cities was and is conducted on an international stage. Early contributions were published in Germany and Switzerland after World War I and in the 1930s.[2] If we go back to Leopold von Ranke and read his *History of Germany in the Period of the Reformation* (1839–1847), we observe that this historian had a clearer vision of the problem than many of his German pupils and followers. He perceived and emphasized three facts of fundamental significance: 1) Urban Reformations united themselves with democratic movements. 2) The Reformation strengthened the awareness of common political, economic, and social interests within urban society. 3) The urban Reformation brought the anti-clerical policies of the city governments (which in the late Middle Ages had prevailed practically everywhere) to their climax.[3]

The present debate was opened by Bernd Moeller's book on *Imperial Cities and the Reformation* whose original German version appeared in 1962.[4] It has been followed by a considerable number of monographs on individual German cities, some of them written by noted British and American authors.[5] The discussion has not yet led to dramatic conflicts of interpretation. There are differences of emphasis, it is true, but the general situation is characterized by careful comparison of local particularities and by the recognition of basic similarities. Ranke's insights have not yet been rejected. The general assumption still seems to be that the cities, and especially the free imperial cities, were the most fertile soil for the Reformation particularly in its beginning stages before the princes assumed political leadership for or against the ecclesiastical renewal and initiated the religious wars.

In the international debate on the Reformation as an urban movement the city of Basel has not been treated very extensively up to now. Although there is general agreement that Basel was an important center of cultural life and commerce all through the sixteenth century, the background of its religious transition in the 1520s has not been widely discussed in recent literature. This neglect can easily be explained.

Research on the history of Basel during the Reformation period has concentrated mainly on the political and intellectual developments. The constitution and the foreign relations of the late medieval city republic are relatively well known. A great deal of work has been done on the development of humanism, on the University, and on the printing industry. Many scholars have studied the religious relations between Basel and other centers of the Reformation, the intellectual impulses which linked the city on the upper Rhine to many places in Western and Central Europe, and the reasons why it became a haven of rest for a large number of religious refugees. The *"histoire événementielle"* of the beginnings and of the breakthrough of the Reformation in Basel has been very carefully studied and described. Among the most important authors are Rudolf Wackernagel whose *Geschichte der Stadt Basel* (3 volumes, 1907–1924) is still indispensable, and Paul Roth who after Emil Dürr's early death finished the publication of the *Aktensammlung zur Geschichte der Basler Reformation* (6 volumes, 1921–1950) and wrote a number of valuable monographs.[6]

What we do not have as yet is an adequate number of studies on the social and economic aspects of the history of Basel during the Reformation period. The medieval centuries have received more attention in this respect, and the same is true of the seventeenth and eighteenth centuries as well as of the period of industrialization. The sixteenth century still offers a fair number of research opportunities, and it presents an exacting task to historians of our time.

Quite recently this task has begun to be tackled. A team of younger scholars has come together in the History Department of the University of Basel, and several dissertation projects have been started in the hitherto neglected field of local history. Among the most important topics are the role of the guilds in the religious upheaval,[7]

the secularization of the monasteries, the social position of the reformed clergy, the reaction of the city council against political and
social dissent and the printing of pamphlets.[8] So much for the present research situation. It is undoubtedly much too early to undertake a general survey of the socio-economic history of Basel in the
early sixteenth century, and our own remarks in no way aspire to
such a thing. They will not present final solutions, but rather point
out some directions in which present research is proceeding and
future work will have to proceed. At the present moment it seems
most important to ask the right questions in order to receive usable
answers. Whenever we venture generalizations, they are tentative
and must be taken as such.

Basel took a relatively long time to become a Protestant city. Almost ten years passed from the first stirrings of religious dissent to
the establishment of the Reformed state church. The beginnings can
be observed in the printing industry. In 1518 the first Basel editions
of Luther's writings were published. From then on their number increased constantly until the early 1520s. At that time the city on the
Rhine became the center of distribution of Luther's works not only
for Southwestern Germany and Switzerland but at least temporarily
for the whole of Western Europe. Several printers, including
Froben, began to publish the writings of the German reformer in
1518, but the leading figure in the great commercial venture was
Adam Petri, the nephew of Johannes Petri whom we have mentioned as one of the great bookprinters in pre-Reformation Basel.
Adam Petri had settled in the city at the beginning of the sixteenth
century. In 1507 he acquired citizenship and began to work as an independent printer. His firm flowered for twenty years. Unlike
Froben he did not specialize in scholarly books. Along with such
printers as Thomas Lamparter and Pamphilus Gengenbach (who
was also a prolific author of ballads, songs, satirical poems, and
plays) Adam Petri began as a publisher of popular literature. He became the main producer of Luther's writings and also brought out
pamphlets of other Protestant propagandists such as Johann Eberlin
von Günzburg. With the help of such scholars as Conrad Pellican he
printed Luther's German Bible. Froben never published a German
book, but Adam Petri's publications are almost exclusively in the
vernacular.[9]

First evidence for the propagation of Protestant ideas among the
population did not appear before 1520, but then it gained strength

very quickly. In several churches, including the cathedral, evangelical sermons began to be preached, and unrest also arose in some of the monasteries. This was particularly true for the Franciscan monastery which at that time stood under the authority of its learned guardian, Conrad Pellican. It is quite obvious that the Basel Reformation movement had been inspired by Luther's books and pamphlets.[10] The writings of Huldrych Zwingli were also discussed as soon as they became known.[11] In 1522 the outward signs of general unrest became abundant. Lenten rules were broken, processions disturbed, and heated debates broke out in many circles. On Palm Sunday (April 13), a dinner party was held at the Klybeck castle, a merchant's residence in Kleinbasel. One course of the meal was a sucking pig. Several members of the lower clergy attended this function. Most prominent among them was Wilhelm Reublin, a university-trained theologian who held the post of "Leutpriester" at the monastery and parish church of St. Alban's. Two months later, on Corpus Christi Day, the same Reublin marched in a procession; but instead of his church's relics he carried the Holy Scriptures. This demonstration of open resistance against the ecclesiastical order offended the government, and in the summer Reublin was banished from the city.[12] He went as a preacher to Witikon near Zürich and eventually became a prominent Anabaptist leader.[13] There were other dissenting priests and monks in Basel, but none of them assumed true leadership. Reublin could well have become the reformer of the city had he behaved a little more cautiously during the early phase of the religious renewal. In the fall of 1522 Johannes Oecolampadius arrived in Basel as a refugee. Since he was indeed to become the leader of the Reformation movement in the city republic, it seems appropriate here to take a look at his earlier career.[14]

He was born in the Swabian town of Weinsberg (near Heilbronn) in 1482. His father, Johannes Husschin (or Hussgen) had been a well-to-do citizen; his mother had come from Basel. At the age of 17 he enrolled in the University of Heidelberg where he became acquainted with the South German humanist reform movement led by Jacob Wimpfeling. After a brief journey to Italy he continued the study of theology in Heidelberg. From 1506 to 1508 he tutored the palatinate princes at Mainz, then finished his studies, took holy orders and in 1510 began to preach regularly at Weinsberg where a prebend had been created for him. While on a generously granted leave of absence he began to study Greek and Hebrew in Tübingen and Stuttgart. Among his teachers was Johannes Reuchlin. During this period (1513–1515) he also met Melanchthon and established a life-long friendship with Wolfgang Fabritius Capito. When in the summer of 1515 Capito moved to Basel as a professor of theology and a cathedral preacher, Oecolampadius followed him and took up work as a corrector in Johannes Froben's printing firm. In the winter of 1515/16 he assisted Erasmus with the edition of the Greek New Testament. After another brief period of residence in Weinsberg he accepted the post of penitentiary of the cathedral at Basel in 1518, but shortly afterwards he was appointed cathedral preacher in Augsburg. Before he went there the University of Basel conferred upon him the doctorate in theology.

In Augsburg Oecolampadius suddenly found himself in the midst of the heated debates about Luther's writings. He was favorably impressed by them because they confirmed his own views about the necessity of ecclesiastical renewal, but the tension between his humanist ideas of reform and Luther's much harsher criticism of the Roman Church created much insecurity in his mind. In order to find clarity he left his post and entered the Birgittine monastery of Altomünster in Bavaria as a monk. Here he wrote two tracts, one on Luther's teaching and the other on Confession. They showed that he had broken with the Catholic tradition and that he had embraced the doctrine of justification by faith alone. The two pamphlets were published in 1521 and caused a great deal of unrest among the monastic community.[15] Oecolampadius had to flee from Altomünster. He became chaplain to Franz von Sickingen on the Ebernburg near Frankfurt, but he did not feel secure there and in November 1522 left for Basel.

He was already well-known and had many friends among the scholars. It was not Froben but Andreas Cratander who now employed him as a corrector and allowed him to resume the translations of patristic texts which he had begun before going to Augsburg. Soon Oecolampadius began to correspond with Zwingli. In the spring of 1523 he gave his first lecture course at the University and started to preach at St. Martin's. His first academic course was a commentary on Isaiah, and because he lectured partly in German, his success was quite extraordinary. Against the opposition of some conservative members of the University the city council appointed him professor of theology along with Conrad Pellican.[16]

It has been rightly said that in his double position as teacher and preacher Oecolampadius was able to consolidate the Reformation movement and to set it upon a sound theological basis,[17] but in spite

of his success he never attained an authority comparable to that of
Zwingli in Zürich. The climax was still far away, and when it came,
Oecolampadius did not stand in the center of events.[18]

During the year 1523 the lines between the parties began to be
firmly drawn. On the conservative side stood the majority of the
University professors, the cathedral clergy, the bishop, and a politically influential group of wealthy merchants. Around Oecolampadius rallied some parish priests, a number of reform-minded
monks and the great majority of the artisans. The city government
tried to mediate and to avoid rash decisions. In the spring of 1523 it
issued a decree which ordered all preachers to base their sermons on
the Bible alone and not on the writings of Luther "and other doc-
tors."[19] Several public disputations followed, but they lacked the
decisive character of those held in Zürich.[20]

In 1525 the peasants of the "Landschaft" rose against the city, and
Anabaptist missionaries began to recruit followers inside its walls as
well as in the country.[21] The mounting crisis caused the Little Council to incline more and more toward conservatism. At the same time,
however, it began to prepare the secularization of the monasteries.[22]
On All Saints' Day Oecolampadius ventured to replace the mass by
an evangelical communion service.[23] In a treatise on the Eucharist
which he had written a few weeks earlier he revealed that his sym-
bolic understanding was very close to Zwingli's doctrine. Here
Oecolampadius clearly opposed Luther, but he was also criticized
by Erasmus from whom he had alienated himself since his stay in
Augsburg. The issue was so controversial that Oecolampadius had to
publish his little book in Strasbourg.[24] Lengthy discussions followed
again, but the Little Council did not take sides. By the end of 1525
five of the six city parishes were led by ministers of the new faith.
Now the population was completely split, but in spite of increasing
tension the Council continued to sit still. In 1527 and 1528 it issued
two new decrees which proclaimed freedom of the faith for everyone. Though these statements sound very progressive to the modern
reader they were not motivated by a generally accepted concept of
religious toleration, but rather by a desperate hope that the conflict
would eventually calm down and disappear.[25] No one wanted coexistence, however. The aim of both parties was total victory and
elimination of the opposing opinion, but hope for a peaceful settle-
ment was naturally cherished by those interested in the preservation
of the social and political order. A city shaken by internal turmoil
could not keep its prosperity.

During the year 1528 it became more and more obvious that the progress of the Reformation could not be stopped. On December 23, 1528 an informal assembly of guild members drew up a petition in which the Little Council was urged to take a final decision in favor of the establishment of the new church.[26] This signalled the breakthrough. From now on the Reformation was entirely the guilds' affair. They started negotiations with the Council and with the mediators who had arrived from the other Swiss cantons and from Strasbourg to help avert a civil war. This went on for several weeks. When the Council failed to declare itself in favor of the religious change, the guilds finally took action against it. On February 8, 1529 they organized a mass meeting near the cathedral and confronted the Council with an ultimatum. On the next day, while they were still waiting for the final answer, a riot erupted and led to an ugly episode of iconoclasm. The Council could no longer remain silent. The mass, and with it the whole Catholic worship, was abolished. All monasteries were taken over by the secular government. Twelve council members who had opposed the Reformation to the very last were forced to resign, and a constitutional change was brought about which will have to be discussed later-on.[27] On April 1, 1529 the new church order was issued, the so-called *Reformationsordnung*. This was the foundation upon which the new Reformed church within the old city state was to grow and thrive.[28]

Our very sketchy summary of the history of the Basel Reformation has deliberately stressed the religious, the ecclesiastical and—in one prominent case—the biographical aspects. We shall now try to widen our field of vision by examining some of the connections between the spiritual and the material factors which determined this general development. In order to do this with reasonable brevity we must limit ourselves to a small number of specific facts. First we shall consider some events which happened in the year 1521. Then we shall discuss the troubles of 1525, and finally we shall proceed to the revolutionary upheaval of 1529.

1521 was a very eventful year for the inhabitants of Basel. Erasmus came back to stay, evangelical preachers began to propagate the new faith, the town hall was finished, and Hans Holbein the Younger was commissioned to embellish it with a number of murals. Although the religious question did not yet occupy everyone's mind, many other conflicts among the population caused a general feeling of uneasiness and insecurity.[29]

The removal of the bishop's influence on the elections of the city government was a radical and unilateral departure from an old tradition which did not find general approval. It was obvious that the Council's decision would have two results: it would lead to a general secularization of city politics and increase the power of the guilds.

Another element of unrest emanated from the problems of foreign policy. Here Basel sat in the same boat with the other Swiss cantons. Since 1516 when perpetual peace had been concluded, the King of France entreated the Confederation to supplement the treaty with a defensive alliance. This alliance would give him the right to recruit Swiss mercenaries whenever his country was under attack. Because the Diet stood under similar obligations to the Pope and had also been approached in the same matter by the Emperor, there was considerable resistance against the French alliance. Francis I tried to break this resistance by showering private pensions upon influential politicians, and he eventually succeeded. While Swiss troops were still in the papal service, the alliance with France came into effect in the spring of 1521. Only Zürich refused to sign it.[30] In most cantons the rivalries between the friends of France, those of the Emperor, and those of the Pope immediately escalated. In Basel the situation was worsened by the fact that private pensions from France whose acceptance had been forbidden up to now were no longer shunned but greedily accepted. Several cases of corruption became known and created an atmosphere of suspicion and mistrust. The majority of the population sympathized with the Emperor. The friends of France and the recipients of pensions were less numerous but generally wealthy and powerful. More than once popular riots against the "Kronenfresser" ("crown eaters") threatened to break out and some of these men were eventually convicted and forced to resign from the Little Council. Again, the guilds asserted themselves successfully by conducting a general vote among all their members which once again forbade the acceptance of private pensions.[31]

1521 was a turbulent year indeed. In addition to the emerging religious controversy, the constitutional struggle between the city government and the bishop, and the disagreements about the French alliance, a fourth conflict developed between artisans and merchants. The history of this socio-economic antagonism was already long and complicated. A climax had been reached in the 1490s, and now the conflict gained momentum again. Like the controversy against the French alliance it showed that the guilds were not united in their political intentions. The wealthy tradesmen of the "gentlemen's guilds" who had risen to political leadership, shamelessly used their power to further their own business interests. Against this tendency the artisans protested vehemently. The fact that some of the "gentlemen" had greatly profited from the French pensions combined the two controversies with each other. The opposition to the commercial elite in the "gentlemen's guilds" was led and supported by the craft guilds. Its effect was quite extraordinary: The Little Council invited all the guilds to state their grievances.[32] While the merchants declared themselves satisfied with their situation, the artisans submitted a very long list of complaints. Most of these complaints applied to the monopolistic activities of the merchants and to the competition from outside the city. Connections with the rising religious conflict became visible in the rather frequent complaints about the economic activities of the monasteries. The monasteries could produce craft goods without being subject to guild regulations. They could work at cheaper rates than the city artisans and were therefore considered intolerable competitors. Among the occupational groups who voiced such protests were the wool weavers, the masons, the carpenters, the coopers, and the cabinet makers.[33]

The Council reacted to the artisans' grievances with considerable energy. It prepared a new "Gewerbeordnung" (Trade constitution) which was put into force after much discussion in 1526. This constitution made it impossible for the merchants to sell imported goods that could also be produced in Basel. It gave the artisans their own sales monopoly in the city and its territory and forbade the monasteries to produce and sell craft goods. On the whole it showed that the craftsmen had gained an important, if not a final, victory over the merchants.[34]

1525 was the year of the peasants' uprising in the Basel territory. On May 3 they marched upon the well-armed city, but were stopped at the closed gates. Their demands were similar to the famous Twelve Articles of the German peasants. The city government reacted with restraint, promised concessions, and with the help of mediators from Solothurn induced the peasants to return to their villages. Charters of liberty were then issued to every district, and peace was restored after about four weeks. The Basel peasants became so submissive again that in 1532 the city could revoke all its concessions without any further protest from them.[35]

While the peasants' uprising lasted, however, there were critical moments for the authorities because it was paralleled by another tumult inside the city walls. This event is less well known than the peasants' movement, but it is not without interest. For the first time in the history of the Basel Reformation we can observe a commotion led by a clearly identifiable social group and unleashed by a combination of religious and socio-political motives. Whether there had been any cooperation with the peasants we do not know, but this question is of minor importance. The movement within the city was led by the weavers' guild.[36] This was one of the smaller craft corporations. Most of its members were poor. The tax registers of the fifteenth century show that the weavers' average income had always been lower than that of most other artisans, while as in other cities, they were particularly affected by economic fluctuations. Their social status was comparatively low, and most of them lived in the "Steinenvorstadt," a lower-class section of the city. It is an established fact that Reformation propaganda won its first adherents among the poor inhabitants of the "Vorstädte" which lay outside the old city walls but inside the fortifications erected during the fifteenth century. Most Basel chronicles of the Reformation and Post-Reformation era emphasize the staunch Protestant attitude of the people in the "Steinenvorstadt."[37] The manifestation of their open dissent had begun in the winter of 1524/25 when they placed a declaration before the Council—the author being most probably a cleric—in which they proclaimed that they were no longer willing to pay for their guild's altar lamp in the cathedral. For this decision they gave two reasons, one religious, the other practical. They stated that burning oil had nothing to do with spreading the word of God, and that the costs for the oil were so high that many of the guild's members could not buy enough food for themselves and their families.[38]

The latter statement was clearly an exaggeration. From the relevant account-books we know that those who paid for the altar lamp were not ordinarily the poor guild members of the "Steinenvorstadt," but wealthy cloth merchants who belonged to the gentlemen's guilds and kept up a second membership in the weavers' guild. Double guild-membership was lawful in Basel.[39] It enabled the merchants to exercise their political influence among the artisans, and to keep them under control. Naturally the craft guilds had always tried to abolish double membership but without lasting success. The decision of the weavers to give up the altar lamp was thus part of the social conflict of the time and it must be seen as a covert attack by the artisans against the merchants.

We do not know how the weavers' message was received by the

Council or what happened within their guild in the early spring of 1525, but it seems that unrest prevailed in the Steinenvorstadt during most of this period. On April 30 the preacher Marx Bertschi gave a sermon in the nearby St. Leonhard's church which must have included some very harsh remarks about the city's ruling class, for he was later officially reprimanded. On the same day, open riots broke out in the Steinenvorstadt and quickly spread to the other suburbs. News of the peasants' uprising increased the tension and there was talk about opening the gates and breaking into the monasteries. Before any such thing happened, however, the Council was able to quell the tumult and restore order. During the investigations which were conducted afterwards it became known that one Ulrich Leiderer, a weaver and clothier, had drawn up and distributed a number of revolutionary articles in which he had demanded several constitutional changes and the removal of fifteen Catholic members from the Little Council.[40] Such a purge was to happen in 1529, but now the time did not yet seem ripe.

Although the sources do not reveal much about the city riots of 1525, they show that its leaders were radical adherents of religious and political change. Both aims were pursued at the same time and by the same representatives of the lower social strata.

We now pass to the decisive events of 1529. In their petition of December 23, 1528 the guilds had touched upon the religious issue only. During the first weeks of the new year, however, the demand for constitutional change came again to the foreground. In the morning of February 8, eight hundred guild members gathered in the church of the Franciscans. They elected a committee to go before the Little Council and present the proposals for ecclesiastical and political renewal. The religious demands have already been mentioned. The political demands involved two main points: 1) The masters and aldermen of the guilds should no longer be elected by the "Zunftvorstände" but by all members. 2) The Little Council should henceforth be elected every year by the Great Council. These proposals were quite revolutionary. They revealed the general intention to establish a democratic government of the guilds and to put an end to the rule of an oligarchic elite.[41] It is understandable that the Little Council was terrified and paralyzed. The ultimatum to abolish Catholic worship and to expel the twelve Catholic council members was bad enough, but the political demands may have been considered even more dangerous. While the negotiations went on, the above-mentioned mass meeting took place. The town hall was virtually under siege, the population in arms. Then the iconoclasm came. Although it is mentioned in many contemporary sources, we do not know to what extent guild members were involved. That some of them took an active part in the work of destruction cannot be doubted. The open revolt did not last more than a few hours, but that was long enough to induce the Council to give in to all the demands that had been brought before it.[42]

If we look at the events which immediately followed the storm of February 9, it is apparent that the victory of the guilds was incomplete. The religious renewal was achieved, but certainly not the realization of political democracy.

What the iconoclasm had begun violently was completed systematically within a few days. All the remaining images were burned and the church treasures confiscated. One week after the upheaval the insides of all the churches of Basel were empty and whitewashed. Protestant worship services were held everywhere in the city and also in the villages of the "Landschaft."[43] While the preachers began to work on the new church order, the laymen began to draw up the new political constitution. On February 12 an assembly convened that was to function as something like a constitutional convention. It consisted of the remaining members of the Little Council, the Great Council, and four supplementary delegates from each guild, a total of about three hundred men altogether. The first decision contained a pledge to protect general peace and security within the city community. The assembly then decreed an amnesty for everything that had happened during the riots and stated its intention to establish a new electoral system.[44]

At this point a general change of direction became visible. The democratic tendency which had characterized the guilds' politics until the final establishment of the Reformation suddenly faded away. The community was requested to promise in advance that it would accept all the decisions of the constituent assembly, and without a single exception the guilds hastened to declare their submission. Now the new constitution ("Ratsordnung") was drafted, but it soon became clear that what was decided now did not at all correspond to the guilds' demands of February 8. The franchise of the guilds' members remained strictly limited to internal affairs. The assembly decided that the representatives of the guilds in the two Councils should be elected by the executive committees alone. Eligibility, moreover, was limited. Public office was open only to those who explicitly professed adherence to the new faith.[45]

Four years later, in 1533, the rights of the citizens were even further restricted. The election of the guild masters was now reserved to the executive committees of the guilds and that of the "Häupter" to the Little Council. Furthermore, the yearly election of that body by the Great Council was abolished again and replaced by the traditional custom of cooptation. Thus the city of Basel, now a center of Protestantism, returned to an oligarchic system of government.[46]

Oecolampadius had died on November 23, 1531. Less than two months earlier Zwingli had lost his life on the battlefield of Kappel where Zürich and the other Protestant cantons had been decisively defeated by the Catholics. We have seen how Oecolampadius became the leader of the Basel Reformation and how until 1525 he brought his movement into far-reaching doctrinal harmony with the teaching of the Zürich reformer. Now we must look back once more at his role in the establishment of the new ecclesiastical order at Basel.

Oecolampadius was highly respected by his adherents. He was undoubtedly a courageous man and the most knowledgeable theologian among the reformed preachers, but he was not a charismatic leader. Although like most other Church reformers he considered himself an instrument of God and believed that there was only one evangelical truth which ought to govern the Christian community, he was not a militant fighter. He remained a scholar and preacher who hoped to convince his adversaries through the zealous propagation of the word of God. He did not like open confrontation, and he loathed violence. He was much concerned about the irreversible escalation of the religious and political conflicts, but his warnings were to no avail.

When the struggle reached its dramatic climax on February 8/9, 1529, Oecolampadius remained in the background, but as soon as the storm was over he became active again in helping create the new constitution of the Church. The Protestant "Reformationsordnung" was declared in force by the Little and the Great Councils on April 1, 1529. Shortly afterwards Oecolampadius appeared as the first Protestant preacher in the cathedral, the first "Antistes" of the Reformed Basel Church.[47] He continued to be its leader after its official establishment, and was generally recognized as such.

It is impossible to summarize here the theological ideas of Oecolampadius. For our present purposes it is enough to say that they were very close to those of Zwingli. One point, however, deserves to be mentioned: Since his days as a cathedral preacher in

Augsburg, Oecolampadius had never ceased to reflect on the problem of church discipline. For obvious reasons this problem was of paramount importance for every Protestant reformer who broke with Catholicism, and when the new order had been established in Basel, Oecolampadius came back to it. Unlike other reformers he did not want to lay the authority over Church discipline and particularly the power of excommunication exclusively into the hands of the preachers. Therefore, in a speech before the Council he proposed the creation of an office of lay presbyters who should watch over the moral life of the church members and together with the clergy decide on the punishment of sinners.[48] This suggestion was discussed at length by the Little Council, but then rejected.[49] Church discipline was to remain under the authority of the magistrate. Oecolampadius was not successful in introducing a presbytery or "consistoire" into the Basel Church, but the idea was taken up in Strasbourg, and it was to become a very important element in Calvin's organization of the Church of Geneva.

Looking at the Reformed State Church of Basel after 1529 we can observe a general development similar to that of the secular constitution of the city republic, namely a definite return to conservatism. The Little Council had taken over the authority of the bishop and was not at all willing to grant any independence to the church. The two constitutive foundations were the "Reformationsordnung" of 1529 and the Basel Confession of 1534.[50] The city was divided into four parishes, the workship services and their liturgy were organized, and marital affairs were controlled by a marriage court ("Ehegericht"). Twice a year the preachers had to attend synods during which their theological knowledge as well as their moral behavior was examined. In the churches hymns were sung in German, the children had to attend catechetical instruction, and for adults, all church services were compulsory. The whole citizenry was sworn to the Basel confession. This was the complete integration of church and state. Anabaptist tenets were banned. In fact, the persecution of Anabaptists that had begun in 1527 was now taken up again and reached the climax of its brutality in 1530/31 when practically the whole Anabaptist movement of the "Landschaft"—which had never been very strong anyway—was completely stamped out. Oecolampadius was not among the persecutors, but he did nothing to stop their zeal.[51]

Thus in the early 1530s the "Basilea reformata" appears as a strictly ruled and uniformly disciplined Reformed community, both in its secular and ecclesiastical structures. We shall see, however, that this situation did not last very long.

In this chapter I have been able to sketch only a very fragmentary picture of the Reformation in Basel. Several aspects have had to be left out because our research has not yet gone far enough, but some basic points may nevertheless have become clear. After studying the interaction of the different historical forces the most important insight seems to be that in Basel like in other Swiss and German cities the Reformation emanated from a coincidence of factors. The preaching of the word of God fulfilled the religious needs of the people and was therefore of primary importance. In Basel, as elsewhere, the striving for economic and political change which may also be defined as the democratic intentions of particular social groups did not originate in the Reformation period. These manifestations of political dissent came out of the Middle Ages and amalgamated now with the forces of religious dissent. That, I think, can very clearly be observed, and we can also see very well how the connections between religious and socio-political ideas of reform became closer and closer through the 1520s. A third factor which I mentioned only in passing is, of course, the influence of humanism on the development of the religious renewal. Many Basel humanists were most unhappy, it is true, with the course of events in this city of printers and scholars. With his departure to Freiburg in 1529, Erasmus set the most famous but by no means the only example of this negative reaction. On the other hand we cannot overlook the fact that almost all the theological leaders of the Basel Reformation were humanist scholars by training.

There remains the question as to who were the actual spokesmen of popular Reformation propaganda. During the crisis of 1528/29—as we have seen—Oecolampadius did not play a prominent role. Even before that time he had never dominated the scene as a popular leader of religious renewal like Zwingli in Zürich. The study of the weavers' unrest in 1525 shows that the preaching of a man like Marx Bertschi at St. Leonhard's must have provided decisive impulses to those who led the uprising. Various documents from the 1520s point to the popular impact of other parish preachers or former monks who now spread the new doctrine. Among them were Wolfgang Wissenburg, Johann Lüthart, and Thomas Girfalk, to name only a few. About most of these minor leaders of the Reformation movement very little is known.[52] They are mentioned repeatedly in official documents and in contemporary chronicles, but their sermons are not preserved, they published little or nothing, and they left no manuscript writings. Bertschi is somewhat better known than most of the others, because some of his letters to prominent contemporaries have been preserved and can now be found in modern source editions.[53] Wissenburg became a professor of theology after 1531; he was highly respected as a scholar and served three times as rector of the university.[54] Interesting as these facts may be to the student of the history of Basel after the breakthrough of the Reformation, they are not very relevant in our present context. All we can say at the moment is that between 1521 and 1529 some of these little-known preachers must have had a very strong impact upon the middle and lower classes of the population who did not or could not read propaganda literature and theological writings. The sermons of these men must have been as inspiring and perhaps more inspiring even than those of Oecolampadius himself.

These aspects of the Reformation as an urban movement can also be studied in other German and Swiss cities. The coincidence of factors that we observe in Basel is not unique, nor is the fact that the Reformation was initiated from below and not from above.[55]

The question of what was characteristic in the case of Basel is very difficult to answer. We are unable to draw systematic comparisons with other cities because we still do not know enough about the social, economic and political background of the Basel Reformation. Three things, however, may be emphasized: The relatively long duration of the process, the very important role of the guilds, and the movement toward re-oligarchization once the establishment of the new ecclesiastical order was achieved. The long duration was certainly due to the facts that Basel never had a Reformation leader like Zwingli and that opposition against the Reformation was naturally more persistent in an episcopal see than in a town without a bishop. The prominent role played by the guilds cannot be explained without taking into consideration the economic and constitutional history of Basel in the late Middle Ages. All through the fifteenth century, and especially toward its end, the guilds had fought to gain political influence, and they had succeeded on several occasions well before the time of the Reformation. The movement toward re-oligarchization after the victory of the Reformation seems to have been more radical in Basel than in either Zürich or Bern, but it may be comparable to the course of events in Strasbourg after the crisis of 1524/25 as well as in the 1560s and 1570s.[56] It must be borne in mind, however, that both the socio-political structure of the urban community and its general development during and after the Reformation were much more complicated in Strasbourg than they were in Basel.

In the general context of the Reformation as an urban movement the case of Basel does not seem to stand out as exceptional. This assumption will probably remain valid even after considerable progress of specialized research. On the other hand we may also assume that further study of the Basel Reformation will confirm many basic insights that have been gained in the study of the same event in other cities.

Basilea Reformata: The Second Flowering of Humanism: Urban Society and Culture in the Post-Reformation Era

The topic of this chapter is not easy to discuss. Some of its aspects are fairly well known, but a number of crucial problems have not yet been sufficiently studied. The history of the city republic of Basel in the post-Reformation era is not dominated by a single fact or by a series of facts around which everything else can be grouped. Although much research has been done on this period in recent years, the results have been rather fragmentary, and a coherent picture has not yet emerged. There is no comprehensive source collection such as the one edited by Dürr and Roth on the Reformation period (ABR). Rudolf Wackernagel's *Geschichte der Stadt Basel* stops in 1529, and the shorter surveys which were published more recently, are all rather brief and vague on the later sixteenth century.[1]

In spite of this it cannot be doubted that the history of the "Basilea reformata" from the 1530s to around 1600 is full of interesting facts and challenging problems. Some intellectual achievements of the period are rightly counted among the highlights of the city's entire history. As I pointed out in the preface, Basel became a focal point of the late Renaissance for the second time between 1550 and 1580. As in the time of Erasmus the city again attracted an extraordinary number of foreign visitors and sent intellectual impulses to other cultural centers of Europe. An important part of this chapter will be devoted to the city's role as a meeting place of scholars from many countries and as an emporium of ideas. In it I shall discuss the following problems: first I shall try briefly to characterize the policy of the Basel government in regard to foreign visitors and refugees; then I shall turn to a phenomenon that we have become accustomed to call the continuity of humanist ideals in the confessional age.[2] In the third part of my account I shall discuss some aspects of the development of the Basel Reformed Church on its way toward High Orthodoxy, and in the fourth part I shall point to some problems of documentation and source study. Here I shall mention the religious refugees again, and refer to the very great number of unidentifiable foreigners who passed through Basel between 1540 and 1600. I shall also deal with political, religious, intellectual, and social problems throughout and hope to show that they are all very closely related to each other and that they cannot be treated separately.

We have seen that the Reformed church order of 1529 imposed a very strict regime on the people of Basel and that the political constitution drafted after the breakthrough of the Reformation was mainly characterized by the restoration of the oligarchic system.

On the other hand, it cannot be overlooked that the Little Council did not always enforce the ecclesiastical discipline with great energy. As far as prominent citizens or visitors were concerned the government could show surprising leniency. Thus it was possible for Bonifacius Amerbach to refuse to partake of the Lord's Supper according to the Reformed order for four years without losing his influencial post as legal counsel to the city government and professor of jurisprudence.[3] Six years after the breakthrough of the Reformation, Erasmus came back from Freiburg and was enthusiastically welcomed. When he died about one year later the Reformed Antistes Oswald Myconius (the successor of Oecolampadius) gave the funeral sermon, and the Dutch humanist was honored with a monument in the cathedral.[4] Small catholic groups continued to exist in Kleinbasel for several decades. The diary of the reformed preacher Johannes Gast reveals some of these groups and shows that a number of former council members and descendants of old families still clung to Catholicism. In 1532 the Carthusian monastery received official permission to continue celebrating mass as long as there were still monks in it.[5] The bishop, now residing in Porrentruy, kept the official title of Chancellor of the University. Because he was an imperial prince the degrees conferred by the University of Basel were recognized throughout the Empire. This was, of course, very much in the interest also of the Protestant University which, after a three year period of partial inactivity, was re-opened in 1532.[6]

After the persecutions of the Anabaptists had abated in the early 1530s it became possible for adherents of radical Protestant doctrines to live in Basel without being disturbed as long as they did not openly criticize the state church and the secular authorities. Conflicts always arose when radical thinkers or writers abandoned their good conduct and began to attack the ecclesiastical or the political establishment. During the trial against the Anabaptist sect of David Joris which in May 1559 ended with the famous burning of the heresiarch's exhumed body, a Dutch witness and non-member of the sect declared that already in the early 1540s he had advised some of Joris' followers that Anabaptists were in principle not tolerated in Basel but ". . . if a man keeps quiet, refrains from spreading false doctrines, and behaves like any other Christian in worship and everyday life, he has nothing to fear."[7]

As in other Protestant centers the number of foreign refugees began to increase very sharply in Basel after 1540. Most of them came from France, Italy, and the Netherlands where systematic persecution of Protestants had already begun. In the 1550s, during the reign of Mary Tudor, a considerable number of English Protestant refugees appeared. The climax of the influx was reached in the decade from 1567 through 1577. Toward 1600 it decreased gradually, but only to increase again at the time of the Thirty years War.

It is not possible here to discuss in detail the significance of the religious refugees for the economic development of Basel in the sixteenth century. I only want to mention the fact that French and Dutch fugitives introduced the trade of lace-making while Italian artisans brought velvet and silk weaving to Basel. Some foreign merchants started projects of international trade which were to exert a considerable influence on later developments even if they were not realized at once.

A fact which we cannot overlook in this context is the extremely cautious and even timid policy of the Basel government in regard to the religious refugees. They were never welcomed with open arms, and only small numbers were allowed to settle down.[8] Increasing reserve was exercised in conferring citizenship upon foreigners after 1540. The most notorious decision of the Little Council was the so-called "Welschenerlass" (= Decree concerning French and Italian refugees) of February 22, 1546. This document stated that every Frenchman or Italian applying for residence should be turned away ". . . unless he be a rich or a skilful man".[9] The official policy clearly tended toward conferring citizenship only upon those foreigners who, by introducing new trades, could contribute to the commercial and economic prosperity of the city without creating competition with the already existing trades. This applied also to bookprinters and to scholars who were interested in acquiring citizenship. The only good thing to be said about the decree of 1546 is that it was never really enforced, but caution and reserve always prevailed vis-à-vis the foreign refugees. There was always fear of competition and suspicion of foreign business practices as well as of religious doctrines which might be incompatible with the Basel confession. The Little Council very reluctantly permitted the French exiles to hold their own worship services after the massacre of St. Bartholomew. The Italian, Dutch, and British refugees never formed official church congregations. Whether this was because they were not allowed to, or because they did not want to, is unknown.

Between the breakthrough of the Reformation and the end of the sixteenth century the total number of conferments of citizenship was approximately three thousand.[10] Among these new citizens are less than two hundred identifiable religious refugees.[11] Considering the fact that the total population of Basel in the second half of the sixteenth century lay between ten and twelve thousand this is indeed very little.[12] One must take into account, however, that a great number of foreigners who lived in Basel at that time never tried to become citizens. Many of them did not fulfill the requirements, and many simply did not want citizenship. This seems to have applied particularly to scholars who worked in the printing houses or taught at the University, and did or could not consider Basel their permanent residence. It is not surprising that with this attitude they did not become fully integrated into urban society. In many cases they remained on the fringes of the city's social life, and this cannot always be explained by the unwillingness of the indigenous to accept them.

In general, however, we have to admit that the Basel refugee policy was extremely exclusive. Not only was citizenship very difficult to acquire, it also happened that refugees were turned away who only sought temporary asylum. Only a small economic and social elite of foreigners were accepted. This state of facts was aptly described by the Basel historian and archivist Andreas Staehelin: "The impact which the foreign refugees had upon the city republic", he said, "did not rest upon quantity, but upon quality alone."[13]

Evidence for the increasing influx of foreign visitors to Basel can also be gained from the matriculation registers of the University. Until about 1570 the Protestant University had regained the international character of its pre-Reformation days. In that same year the French philosopher Petrus Ramus wrote his famous panegyric on the city of Basel. When he said that the University made its name famous throughout Europe he spoke as a grateful visitor. Nevertheless, his statement was more than a rhetorical exercise.[14] A number of noted scholars from several countries had been appointed to professorships, and the student body, though still relatively small, became more and more international. The majority came from South and Southwest Germany. From 1532 through 1600 the matriculation registers contain the names of about 500 Frenchmen, 250 Frisians and Dutchmen, 150 Poles and Lithuanians, 100 Englishmen, 70 Italians and 60 Scandinavians. The total number of registrations amounted to about 5,600, of which about 20 % were non-German-speaking foreigners.[15] It is clear that the reputation of some teachers would not have sufficed to attract so many foreign students. We know that the geographical location of Basel played a significant role because the itineraries of academic wanderers most often coincided with the trade routes, and we also know that the chancellorship of the bishop who was an imperial prince made Basel a good place to seek degrees. The study of the matriculation registers shows, moreover, that many of the foreign visitors who inscribed themselves were not students in the proper sense but travellers who wanted to enjoy the privileges of academic citizenship. Among the registered visitors who are also identifiable as religious refugees we find a considerable number of well-known scholars. For them the main attraction of Basel was obviously not the University but, again, the printing industry.

It was a happy coincidence that when the influx of foreign visitors began to increase, the city had virtually overcome the shocks caused by the Reformation. As a protestant republic Basel became again what it had been at the time of the council and during the first decades of the sixteenth century: a meeting place of scholars from many nations where free exchange of ideas was possible.

The re-opening of the University in 1532 and the new increase in book publishing which occurred after a brief period of recession during the early 1530s, marked the beginning of a new intellectual flowering period. Both in the University and in the printing shops the foreign scholars became increasingly prominent. It may be mentioned in passing that during the year 1535—shortly before the return of Erasmus—John Calvin at the age of 26 years resided in Basel for some time. It was here that he wrote his *Institutio Christianae religionis*. The first edition of this work was printed in Basel by Thomas Platter in 1536. Its fundamental ideas, which were to attain international significance later-on, were not immediately successful in Basel. Their breakthrough was hindered by various opposing forces for a considerable period of time.

The intellectual atmosphere that gradually developed during the 1540s was largely determined by a number of humanist scholars who considered themselves pupils and successors of Erasmus, and by some younger bookprinters whose production soon became more varied than it had been before 1525. Among the humanist scholars the Italian refugees were most prominent. The central figure was Celio Secondo Curione who had become a professor of Rhetoric in 1547. To the same group belonged Sebastian Castellio, the Savoyard scholar who had been Calvin's collaborator in Geneva and after theological conflicts with his master had come to Basel as a printer's corrector. In 1553 Castellio became professor of Greek. Among the Italian refugees many religious problems were discussed, but in a manner which did not please most of the Reformed preachers of the Basel church. The refugee scholars placed ethics before dogmatics and some of them clearly inclined toward universalist and even rationalist opinions. Out of this group came the vehement protest against the burning of the Spanish antitrinitarian Michael Servetus in Geneva on October 27, 1553.[16] As the editor of the book *De haereticis an sint persequendi* (1554) Castellio became the leading advocate of religious toleration. During the late 1550s he had to endure many harsh attacks from the Genevan reformers. He and Curione were also repeatedly molested by the Basel government. But they were successful teachers. They gathered students from many countries who were to spread their unorthodox ideas not only in Germany, France, and England, but notably in Poland and in the Netherlands.[17] In 1553/54 Basel became a stronghold of anti-Calvinist propaganda. The toleration of Calvin's critics in Basel caused a great deal of indignation not only in Geneva but also in other Protestant towns of the Swiss confederation, especially in Zürich.

A few more words must be said about the printing industry during the period from 1530 through about 1580. Its achievements were outstanding in many respects. Of particular importance were the efforts to re-publish a great number of literary and historiographical works of the Italian Renaissance. It has been rightly emphasized that with this remarkable production the whole arsenal of classical knowledge and humanist education was made available in a comprehensiveness never reached before. Undoubtedly the beautiful re-editions satisfied a widespread interest among an educated public. It was good business to print these books. They could be sold, and they were sold. Their success demonstrated a general consciousness of the persistence of intellectual and educational values in spite of religious and political changes. This is what is meant by the continuity of humanist ideals in the age of confessionalism. The phrase was coined by the late Basel historian Werner Kaegi, the biographer of Jacob Burckhardt.[18] After 1530 this continuity manifested itself in various ways in the Basel printing industry. We detect it not only in what might be called "the Basel renaissance of the Italian Renaissance" but also in a strong new interest in editions of the works of ancient and medieval authors and—after 1536— in a great eagerness to preserve the memory of Erasmus. The writings of the Dutch humanist were quoted and commented on in many later Basel publications. The most important monument to his memory was, however, the first edition of the *Opera omnia* published in 1540 by Jerome Froben and Nicolaus Episcopius. This edition was to remain of fundamental significance until the end of the 17th century when Jean Le Clerc published the Leiden edition.

In order to illustrate some of the general observations which I just made I would now like to concentrate on the activities of two particularly productive Basel printers of the post-Reformation era, namely on Johannes Oporinus (Herbster) and Pietro Perna. Oporinus had been born in Basel and was trained as a classical scholar. He had taught Latin and Greek at the University until 1542 when he decided to devote himself exclusively to the printing and publishing business. He brought out a number of works of Reformation theologians but also of radical authors. Until Sebastian Castellio's death in 1563 he published practically all the writings of this author, including the famous *De haereticis an sint persequendi*. In the early years of his business career Oporinus had ventured some even more daring publications such as Guillaume Postel's *De orbis terrae concordia* (1544), a universalistic handbook for missionaries, and the first Latin edition of the Koran (1542). These editions caused a lot of irritation and excited discussion among scholars, but they made the house of Oporinus famous all over Western Europe.[19] Perna had come from Lucca as a refugee in 1542. He had taken over the printing shop of Thomas Platter two years later. In 1557 he became a citizen and a member of the Saffron guild. His publishing firm prospered until the early 1580s. Its production has been studied with particular interest by Italian and Swiss historians in recent years.[20] Perna was the most productive Basel publisher of Italian Renaissance literature, and he was also the protector of the Italian religious refugees who had come to Basel with him or after him.[21] After Curione's death in 1569 he was the undisputed leader of the Italian scholars' colony in Basel. In the 1560s and 1570s practically all Italian emigrants of the second generation went through his house. Some stayed for extended periods of time, others appear only as hurried callers, stopping over on their way to more distant havens of rest in Poland, Moravia, and Transylvania. Among Perna's most prominent collaborators was Fausto Sozzini who later became the leader of the anti-trinitarian Ecclesia minor in Poland. While in Basel during the 1570s he wrote his treatise *De Jesu Christo servatore* and also helped Perna with an edition of Castellio's hitherto unpublished tracts, the *Dialogi quatuor* (1578).[22]

Both Oporinus and Perna also published books on science and medicine. Oporinus' most famous achievement in this field is the edition of *De humani corporis fabrica* by Andreas Vesalius (1543), one of the most widely known handbooks of anatomy of the sixteenth century.[23] Perna went even further. He printed a large number of writings by empirical scientists who attacked the Aristotelian and Galenian traditions. Among these books are the works of Raimundus Lullus, Thomas Erastus and—most important of all—those of Paracelsus. In addition to these publications Perna brought out many books on magic and alchemy. This publishing activity went along with his vigorous support of humanist criticism of the magisterial Reformation. The many-sidedness of Perna's interests has only recently been fully recognized. He now appears to modern historians as a powerful supporter both of evangelical radicalism and of the new tendencies of scientific thought as they began to gain ground in the second half of the sixteenth century. In an abbreviated formula one might say that he prompted the ideas of such contemporaries as Castellio and Paracelsus at the same time. That in the course of his life he also became a defender of religious toleration, is only logical.[24]

It goes without saying that the major Basel printers of the late sixteenth century frequently got into trouble with the city authorities. Some incidents are fairly well known, e.g. the turmoil about Oporinus' Koran edition, the irritation caused by Perna's second edition of Machiavelli's *Book of the Prince* (1580), and the trial which followed the publication of Castellio's *Dialogi quatuor* (1578) in the course of which Perna very unconvincingly declared that he did not know any Latin and therefore could not have known what the book contained.[25] The censorship authorities repeatedly tried to prohibit the publication of books deemed to contain "heretical" ideas or (if this was impossible) to punish the printers. These activities often led to open conflicts and to eruptions of angry protest against church leaders and city magistrates. One of the most famous expressions of extreme annoyance can be found in a letter of Oporinus to a Bernese friend (1565). In a marginal note the printer expressed his opinion that ". . . the devil has cheated us with this new popery."[26]

On the whole, however, book censorship in Basel was rather inefficient.[27] Many things could be printed which would hardly have left the presses in other Protestant cities. Thus Guillaume Farel was quite right when he wrote to Heinrich Bullinger in 1557: "What you did not allow to be published in Zürich, has been published without difficulties in Basel".[28]

Many printers and the majority of their foreign collaborators still stood at the fringes of the urban society. Most citizens mistrusted them and kept away from them. On the other hand, they also had friends and protectors among the educated. Most of these protectors were scholars themselves, such as the jurist Bonifacius Amerbach and his son Basilius, the physician Felix Platter, and Theodore Zwinger, a classical scholar and medical doctor with a strong interest in the natural sciences who was one of Pietro Perna's closest friends. Among these men there was neither intellectual narrowness nor religious uniformity. When in 1580 Michel de Montaigne visited Basel and talked with some of these prominent citizens, he wrote in his diary that he had found a great variety of opinions and beliefs here and that he had even met some scholars who still showed sympathy for the catholic religion.[29]

We now have to turn our attention again to the history of the Basel Reformed Church. From 1553 through 1585 it was under the leadership of Simon Sulzer. He had been born in the Bernese Oberland and had studied in Basel and Strasbourg. As a young man he had travelled widely and also visited Wittenberg. While he stood at the head of the Basel Church its development was characterized by increasing alienation from the other Swiss Protestant churches and particularly from that of Geneva. The first signs of such an evolution had already become visible under Sulzer's predecessor Myconius. The Basel Church refrained from openly supporting Calvin in a number of doctrinal conflicts, and in the Servetus affair it was rather reserved and quiet while, as we have seen, the humanists protested vehemently. In 1554 it became quite evident that Calvin was confronted with two groups of critics in Basel: the radical humanists around Curione and Castellio on the one hand, and Sulzer with his followers on the other. While Calvin and Beza never ceased to condemn the "academic heretics" of Basel in the harshest possible way, they courted Sulzer and tried again and again to draw him over to their side.[30]

Sulzer was clearly intent on bringing Swiss and German Protestantism into closer contact. This desire led him to steer the Basel Church more and more openly toward a Lutheran course. His term of office as Antistes may well be called the Lutheran or Lutheranizing period of the Basel Reformed Church, for he brought many Lutheran practices into the worship services. Among other things he reinstated the use of organs. On a visit to Strasbourg he openly declared his agreement with the Augsburg Confession which led in 1563 to official criticism from the church leaders of Zürich, Bern, and Schaffhausen.[31] Most important, however, was the fact that Sulzer succeeded in convincing the Basel government to reject the Second Helvetic Confession of 1566. The city republic thus refrained from joining this basic confessional union with the other Protestant cantons. Recent investigations of the pertinent archival materials and a careful study of Sulzer's correspondence have shown that he wanted to keep Basel out of the increasing polarization between the Lutheran and the Reformed Churches, and that he was afraid that by joining the Second Helvetic Confession Basel would cut itself off from the neighboring German churches to the North. This was also a personal problem for Sulzer, because in addition to being Antistes of the Basel Church he had—with the official permission of the Basel government—taken over the post of Superintendent of the Lutheran Church of Baden in 1556. The Augsburg Confession was printed in Basel in 1567, and quite obviously Sulzer planned to put the Basel Church under the "Formula Concordiae" and eventually to lead it into the Lutheran camp. He did not, however, succeed.[32]

It is very difficult to determine who were the supporters of Sulzer's Lutheranizing church policy in Basel. He was always criticized by most of the other ministers and had to be very careful in pursuing his plans. It seems that his chief support came from the political elite of the citizenry and especially from the wealthy merchants. In these circles a deterioration of the good relations with the imperial estates was evidently considered very dangerous.[33] The fact was, however, that Sulzer's ecclesiastical policy led to a fatal isolation of Basel from the Protestant cantons of the Swiss league. This became painfully evident in the conflict with Bishop Jacob Christoph Blarer von Wartensee who in 1579 tried to win back his old territorial rights over part of the Basel "Landschaft". The Basel government could not rally the necessary support of the other Protestant cantons in time and had to raise a huge sum of money to pay off the bishop and to protect its territorial possessions.[34]

In spite of its detrimental political consequences Sulzer's church policy was beneficial to the religious refugees and their humanist protectors. Certainly Sulzer did not like the "heretics", but he did nothing to persecute them systematically, and did not try to expell them from the city. In fact he shared their critical attitude vis-à-vis Calvin and his steadily expanding religious movement. The motivations of this critical attitude were certainly very different, but the aim was the same. I would venture to say that this coincidental Anti-Calvinism was an important reason for the fact that late humanism and evangelical radicalism could survive so long in Basel.

Toward the end of the 1570s, however, the general intellectual atmosphere began to undergo a more perceptible change. It started when, in 1575, the Calvinist Johann Jacob Grynaeus was appointed professor of Theology in Basel. This theologian was also a born organizer and leader. He rallied the forces of opposition against Sulzer around himself, and became more and more influential in the political life of the city republic, especially after the crisis of 1579/80. When Sulzer died in 1585 Grynaeus was elected Antistes. He held the post until 1617, and during this time led the Church of Basel back toward Reformed orthodoxy. It has been said that during the 1580s the "Basilea reformata" gradually ceased to be the haven of humanism and Protestant radicalism.[35] Although this is undoubtedly true, we cannot deny that Johann Jacob Grynaeus was instrumental in preserving the international reputation of the city and its University, at least for a considerable length of time.

It is still an open question how the election of Grynaeus to the office of Antistes came about, and the shift in the intellectual atmosphere of Basel around 1580 has not yet been fully explored. We do know that by that time the second flowering of humanism came to an end, and the general toleration of non-conformist opinions gradually disappeared. But it did not happen suddenly. The activities of the printing houses went on, works of classical and Renaissance literature continued to be printed, and philosophical writings as well as books on the natural sciences still found publishers. But everything went a little slower than before and gradually the quantity of new publications decreased. The dominant characteristic of the new period was the consolidation of church discipline and a visible increase in the number of governmental decrees regulating public and private life in the city republic.[36]

Foreign visitors continued to appear in considerable numbers, and there were still many scholars and students among them. Their main objective, however, was no longer the publication of their manuscripts but the study of orthodox Reformed theology at the University. Grynaeus was a highly respected teacher, and he continued to teach after having become Antistes. Also attractive to foreign students were the courses of Amandus Polanus von Polansdorf, a scholar from Silesia who was appointed professor of Old Testament in 1596, and soon became an internationally renowned authority of orthodox Calvinism. Students still came from many countries, but only one national group shall be mentioned here as an example.

Both Grynaeus and Polanus attracted a remarkable number of students from Bohemia and Moravia. Polanus was especially popular among them. In his early years he had served as a private tutor to the young men of the aristocratic Zierotin family. He had also taught and preached at Eibenschitz, the ecclesiastical center of the Moravian Brethren.[37] Students from Bohemia and Moravia had attended the University of Basel for a long time, but after 1585 their number increased quite perceptibly. After their return many among them rose to prominence as ministers and politicians. As in the case of the Poles who had been particularly numerous from 1550 to 1570, there were many sons of the aristocracy among the Bohemians and Moravians. They usually brought a whole retinue of tutors and servants and had them registered in the matriculation books. While the Poles had been particularly attracted by the humanists and by the so-called "heretics", the Bohemians and Moravians felt more at home with the orthodox Reformed professors. Some of them took degrees, others improved their general education or simply enjoyed the pleasures of student life outside the classroom. For all of them Basel was a significant place of temporary residence on their grand tour through Western Europe. Many lasting relationships were established with teachers and friends, and a number of Basel theologians subsequently went to Moravia where they established themselves as teachers and preachers within the Moravian church. The history of mutual relationships can be followed until the outbreak of the Thirty years war.[38]

I should like, however, to remain in the sixteenth century and turn to the problem of sources. The documentary basis of the facts and developments mentioned in this chapter is very complex. It consists primarily of personal records, such as diaries and letters. The records of the University, as well as those of the Basel Church and of the City Councils are also very important. With the exception of the University matriculation registers, no major body of these documentary materials is fully accessible in a printed edition.[39] Most of the unpublished sources are known to specialists, but not all of them—I mentioned this earlier-on—have been systematically explored. It is still possible to find new information on intellectual, political, and social developments in documents which at first sight seem rather unlikely to yield such information. An excellent example is provided by the financial records of the University of Basel, especially the account books of the rectors.[40]

These *Rationes rectoratus* have been studied only superficially until now. Although one would not expect it, they reveal quite a lot of evidence for the historical role of Basel as a center of international cultural activity. The yearly accounts contain lists of expenses for the reception and entertainment of more or less prominent visitors and of the subsidies that were given to little-known or anonymous travellers, scholars, students, and other people who asked for them at the rector's office. In the course of the years these lists steadily increased in length. Looking through them we can see that the University functioned as a meeting place of internationally renowned scholars and other prominent contemporaries. At the same time an ever-increasing number of needy people were supported. For them the University was something like a welfare institution. It fulfilled a function that in an earlier period had been fulfilled by the monasteries.

Most of the identifiable visitors of the University were travelling scholars and students, but quite often princes, foreign diplomats, and Protestant or Catholic church dignitaries were entertained. The hospitality of the University manifested itself in two ways. Prominent guests were usually treated to a formal banquet in one of the city's taverns. These banquets were attended by the rector or one of the deans who functioned as the rector's deputy, and by a number of invited professors. Less prominent visitors received a larger or smaller portion of honorary wine which the University procured from the city government. The anonymous travelers simply received money to enable them to continue their journey. When famous visitors are mentioned in the expense accounts the respective entries often confirm a stay in Basel that was already known from other sources, but this is not always the case. In many instances the account books furnish the only evidence of a visit.

The lists of subsidies given to anonymous persons make it possible for us to survey a long and unbroken column of religious refugees, academic wanderers, and other travelers who thronged the narrow streets of the city throughout the sixteenth century. The traces of this column can also be observed in the weekly accounts of the City Council. In addition the account books of the rectors illustrate the manifold difficulties of destitute travelers, the predicaments of otherwise unknown individuals, and the very real dangers that threatened the simple and defenseless travelers everywhere. Thus the University, while playing the role of a center of international academic contacts, also functioned as an institution of social assistance. It helped to maintain the city's reputation as a place where both intellectual stimulation and material support could be found.

It would be easy to draw up a long list of famous names which appear in the rector's account books, but I must confine myself to a very small number of examples. In the account of the academic year 1535/36 we learn that Erasmus was formally but enthusiastically fêted by the University upon his return to Basel. In the fall of 1548 Johannes Brenz, the reformer of Württemberg, was entertained at a banquet, and shortly afterwards the rector of the (Catholic) University of Freiburg i.Br. received the somewhat lesser honor of a gift of wine. One of the first religious refugees to be formally welcomed was Pier Paolo Vergerio, the former bishop of Capodistria who in 1549 was to become the protestant preacher of Vicosoprano in the Bergell valley.[41] At about the same time the imperial ambassadors Angelo Rizio and Ascanio Marso visited the University. Marso was to become the well-known author of the *Discorso de i Sguizzeri* (1558).[42] In the late 1540s, and especially during the 1550s, an increasing number of Italian refugees were welcomed, including the theologian Pietro Martire Vermigli, the famous jurist Matteo Gribaldi, and Lelio Sozzini, the uncle of Fausto who became an admirer of Castellio.[43] During the reign of Mary Tudor many English protestants came to Basel and joined the academic community. Several among them enjoyed the rector's hospitality, notably Sir John Cheke, the famous Greek scholar from Cambridge who had tutored King Edward VI.[44]

Among the Reformation leaders, Theodore Beza was often received,[45] but Calvin only once.[46] Johannes Sturm from Strasbourg appears several times,[47] and the same is true of Pierre Toussaint from Montbéliard who was one of the most energetic propagators of Castellio's idea of religious toleration.[48]

The outstanding figure among the French guests of the University was François Hotman, the famous author of the *Franco-Gallia*. His first visit is mentioned in the account of 1555/56. He was a staunch Calvinist and liked neither Sulzer nor the humanist critics of Calvin. More than once he suggested that they should be expelled from the city. In spite of his hostility to the radical humanists he came back in 1558 to take his doctoral degree in law, and twenty years later he took up permanent residence in Basel.[49] From then on his name appears frequently in the account books. Although he was not an ordinary member of the faculty, he took part in many banquets and other academic festivities as a very regular guest. If he enjoyed these functions, the University also seems to have been interested in having him around, especially when other French visitors had to be entertained. He could be shown off because he was famous, and, presumably, because his command of the French language was better than that of most Basel professors. When Montaigne visited the city in 1580 Hotman was very much in the foreground as an interlocutor and guide.[50]

More interesting than the testimonies to prominent foreign visitors are the lists of subsidies given to poor and anonymous strangers. In the second half of the sixteenth century (i.e. 1557ff) these lists always appear under the headings "pietatis causa" or "eleemosynae et viatica."

Here we find references to innumerable "studiosi" or "conconiatores pauperes," but also to travelling musicians and actors who were always ready to perform, but who then expected to be paid and fed. The same applies to numerous "poetae" and "auctores" who gave unwanted manuscripts and books to the rector, and then considered themselves entitled to adequate remuneration.[51] Often one reads about "magistri" and "licentiati" who expected help simply because they held academic degrees. Their names are rarely mentioned. Special reference is always made to people who came from far distant countries like Poland, Scotland, Ireland, Spain, or Greece. In one account (1578/79) we even find two men from Cyprus who received some money at the rector's office. Frequently the account books also contain indications as to the reasons for the travelers' poverty. Many of them explained that they had been robbed. Some pretended to have suffered in Russian or Turkish prisons. Others simply stated that they had been driven from their homes because of their religion. Several rectors added their own observations about the people they had to deal with. They described some of the callers as scholarly, honest, and pious, others as unsavory, dirty, or too talkative. Here and there we hear about an actor who looks like a drunkard, a musician with bad manners, a young man who calls himself "magister artium" but appears to be a "homo indoctus" etc., but all these travelers received their gift of money, food, or wine. There are no visible rules as to the quantity of the subsidies. The financial contributions sometimes amount to a few shillings and pennies, sometimes to more than two pounds. Very often one feels that the respective rector was glad to be rid of the more unsavory fellows who had knocked on his door. Quite frequently we read about sick people: the preacher from Bavaria who is so ill that he cannot continue his journey and needs a place in the hospital, the schoolmaster from the Valais whose wife can no longer walk, or the student from Lower Saxony who is learned but melancholy and needs consolation more than money.[52] Again and again one can see from the account books that poor people traveled in groups, and almost every year one comes across a baptized Jew who advertised himself as a teacher of Hebrew.

Toward the end of the sixteenth century the entries under "pietatis causa" become more and more numerous. Some of the rectors started to summarize them, indicating only the total of the expenses. At the end of 1584/85 the then rector Christian Wurstisen, a noted historian and mathematician, remarks that in the course of the academic year he has given subsidies to ninety-four poor students and other travelers, ". . . quorum catalogum taedet adscribere."[53]

It is, of course, impossible to pretend that the anonymous strangers who passed through Basel in the course of the sixteenth century and received financial support from the University, contributed substantially to the city as a cultural center, but they belong to its history like the famous scholars of the time and cannot be ignored. They may well have passed the word that Basel was a place where the destitute and the oppressed might expect hospitality. This judgment was compatible with that of many more prominent refugees.

The city republic on the upper Rhine was attractive to foreigners for many reasons. Among the visitors who settled down and stayed for extended periods were a number of non-conformist thinkers whose ideas pointed in new directions and who were not always understood by the majority of their contemporaries. Their lives were often difficult, and they were involved in all kinds of unpleasant and often dangerous conflicts, but they nevertheless contributed to the town's radiating power as a cultural center. To one of these individuals we shall turn in our next chapter.

Chapter IV

A Momentous Impulse
from Sixteenth Century Basel:
Sebastian Castellio and the Origins
of the Debate on Religious Toleration.

Sebastian Castellio died in Basel on December 29, 1563. The news brought considerable relief to the leaders of the Reformed churches in Switzerland, particularly to those of Zürich and Geneva. At last they were free from the unpleasant radical who for more than twenty years had dared again and again to criticize the measures taken by the Reformed churches against heretical extremists. At last the voice was silenced that had so often attacked the Reformed doctrines of the Kingdom of God and of His revelation.

If it brought relief, the news of Castellio's death also created a great deal of fresh indignation. It became known that the deceased professor of Greek at the University of Basel had been buried with great honors in the cloisters of the cathedral. Even more provoking, however, was another fact: in early January 1564 the bookprinter Johannes Oporinus brought out a little volume that contained a long panegyric on the deceased scholar written in elegant Latin hexameters. The author was one Paul Cherler, a young man from Saxony who had just received the degree of bachelor of arts at the University of Basel. He had studied under Castellio and become his friend. Now he became the first author to praise the character and scholarship of his teacher. Cherler's poem has preserved its value as a historical source. It is the first biography of Castellio, and it contains a considerable amount of information not to be found anywhere else.[1]

Some of the Reformed leaders in Zürich gained the impression that the Basel authorities were in full accord with Cherler's hymn of praise,[2] but they were wrong. They did not, and could not, know that the last weeks of Castellio's life had been darkened by a dangerous intrigue, and that he had had more enemies than friends in Basel. The funeral had been organized by the University as it was customary to do this for every professor who died in office. The tombstone had been paid for by three Polish noblemen who were former students of Castellio, Cherler's poem was published only because Oporinus had been a life-long friend of the deceased scholar.[3]

Many unpleasant things had indeed happened to Castellio shortly before his death. In November 1563 a long pamphlet containing a number of attacks against the humanist had reached the Basel city council. Its author was Adam Bodenstein von Karlstadt, the son of Luther's famous antagonist, and at that time a practicing physician in Strasbourg. In this pamphlet Castellio was described as a Pelagian, a propagator of the Anabaptist doctrine of separation of Church and State, and a secret adherent of the Roman Catholic doctrine of good works. Castellio had often been obliged to defend himself against charges of this kind in the past, but now something new was brought up: Bodenstein pointed out to the Basel magistrate that Castellio had translated Bernardino Ochino's *Dialogi Triginta* from the Italian into Latin. One of these dialogues contained a passage on the Mosaic marriage laws which seemed to approve of polygamy. Because of this passage the famous Italian reformer had been banished from Zürich, and now Castellio had translated the heresies of his Italian friend. This was enough for Bodenstein to prove that the Basel scholar agreed with the blasphemies pronounced there.[4]

As was to be expected, Bodenstein's pamphlet caused great irritation in the Basel government and among the pastors of the Basel church. A thorough investigation was ordered, and had an actual trial taken place, Castellio would probably have been banished from Basel. We now know that he expected this to happen, and that he planned to emigrate to Poland, the country which at that time offered a last exile to many Protestants persecuted for heresy by the established churches.[5] Then, just as he was about to leave, Castellio died. He was only forty-eight years old. Death, as we see, not only brought relief to his enemies, but to Castellio himself, for it took him away from a troubled life of conflicts, misunderstandings, and intrigues that kept his mind in constant tension and gradually consumed his physical powers as well.

We must not overlook the fact that, in the last phase of his life, Castellio had prepared to leave Basel. He had lived there for almost twenty years and found a number of friends, but unlike many other foreign scholars he had never sought to acquire citizenship. He never found the peace to settle and take roots. He remained a stranger, and the townspeople who knew him took him as such. He never learned more than a smattering of the German language.[6]

On the other hand, it can be said without exaggeration that Basel was in many ways a suitable place for Castellio to live. Although the attitude of the magistrates toward unorthodox religious views varied from relatively far-reaching tolerance to occasional suppression, the general situation was definitely more liberal than in either Geneva or Zürich. Intellectual life, as it prevailed around the University and in the bookprinting houses, was still characterized by an open-minded and irenic atmosphere not very different from that which had prevailed in the days of Erasmus. It was this atmosphere and the possibility of finding work as correctors or editors in the printing houses which, in the middle decades of the sixteenth century, attracted so many foreign scholars and religious refugees to Basel. Castellio's contribution to the intellectual development of his age must always be seen against this background. It might not have taken shape as it did, had he lived in another center of the Reformation.[7]

Castellio was born in 1515 in a small village by name of Saint-Martin-du-Fresne, situated in the Northwestern corner of the Duchy of Savoy, not far from the town of Bourg-en-Bresse. Of his parents almost nothing is known, except that they were simple peasants, uneducated, but honest and god-fearing. The name of the family was Châteillon or Châtillon. We do not know where Sebastian received his elementary education, but when he was twenty years old, in 1535, he came to Lyon and enrolled in the "Collège de la Trinité", a newly founded center of humanist scholarship and culture. Here he learned the ancient languages and also Italian. Whether he ever came into contact with the eminent men who at that time dominated the literary life of Lyon, remains unknown. Neither Rabelais nor Clément Marot taught at the "Collège de la Trinité." Incited by some of his fellow students who, like himself, were ardent lovers of Greek poetry, the young scholar changed his name to "Castalio", thereby evoking the memory of the legendary well of the Muses. He only began to use the better-known form "Castellio" in later life, several years after coming to Basel.

He studied in Lyon for five years and there became an expert classicist. During this same period he also became acquainted with the ideas of the Reformation. The year 1540 brought his religious decision. Castellio left the humanist school and went to Strasbourg. Here he met Calvin who was living in the imperial city as a preacher to the French refugee community after his first and unsuccesful attempt to establish the Reformation in Geneva. Calvin was impressed by the bright young Savoyard scholar. For some time the two even lived in the same house. During the decisive period when Calvin prepared his return to Geneva, Castellio was among his most intimate friends and collaborators, and he went to Geneva even before the reformer returned there himself. Shortly after his arrival, Calvin had his young friend appointed rector of the "Collège de Rive." This was the old Latin school of the City of Geneva. It was now reorganized to become the institution which prepared its pupils for the study of theology.

Thus, Castellio occupied a position which imposed great responsibility upon him. The re-organization of the school was to a large extent his work, and one of the results of these pedagogical endeavors was his first literary achievement, the *Dialogi sacri*, a collection of biblical dialogues in Ciceronian Latin.[8]

Friendly relations with Calvin did not last long, however. The philologist Castellio expressed doubts on the origins and religious significance of the Song of Solomon. Furthermore, he had some reservations concerning the way in which Calvin interpreted the doctrine of Christ's descent into Hell. Behind these theological dissensions, a fundamental disunity became evident. On the one side stood the iron-willed Reformer, realistically recognizing the necessity to enforce discipline within his newly-established church and firmly intent on eliminating everything that might threaten its doctrinal unity. On the other side stood the humanist scholar who was not disposed to accept any kind of doctrinal authority that seemed to be incompatible with the text of the Holy Scriptures. Already here we see that to Castellio the individual conscience was more important than collective discipline enforced by human authority.

A compromise was impossible. In 1543, Calvin and the other pastors of Geneva began to turn away from Castellio. When he declared himself disposed to preach the Gospel to those infested with the plague—a job that none of the ministers wished to take upon himself—he was rejected on the grounds that he was not ordained. This and Calvin's refusal to accept him into the ministry led to his decision to leave Geneva. He was not, however, formally and officially banished. Calvin even gave him a letter of recommendation. In this document the points of theological dissension are mentioned, but there is also considerable praise for Castellio's exceptional erudition.[9]

In the fall of 1544 Castellio came to Basel. He soon found employment as a corrector in the printing firm of Johannes Oporinus. Thus began a period of quiet scholarly work, but also of extreme poverty. This period was to last nine years. Besides working on several editions of ancient authors, Castellio undertook two translations of the Bible, one into Ciceronian Latin, the other into popular French. The former was published in 1551, the latter in 1555. In this period of hardship the traditional historical image of Castellio had its origin. It was to be drawn and redrawn by many later authors. It is the image of the poor but hard-working refugee scholar who had to feed his growing family through manual labor as a fisherman and collector of driftwood, and who had all of his children (he left four sons and four daughters) learn a trade in order to support themselves. The documentary basis of this image can be found in some passages of one of Castellio's own writings.[10] Among its most remarkable later reproductions are those in Montaigne's *Essais* and in Pierre Bayle's *Dictionnaire historique et critique*. When Montaigne referred to Castellio's poverty and to the fact that this scholar had found so little contemporary recognition, he went as far as to speak of "the shame of this century".[11]

The most difficult time seemed overcome when, in 1553, Castellio was appointed Professor of Greek at the University of Basel. This appointment had been brought about by Bonifacius Amerbach, the one-time friend of Erasmus who, as a professor of jurisprudence, was still a leading figure in the University. Amerbach had been friendly to Castellio from the beginning. He had extended assistance to him in many ways and had also entrusted him with the education of his son Basilius. Castellio became very much attached to the Amerbach family and always cherished a feeling of deep gratitude toward the venerable Bonifacius.[12] Among the professors of the University he had also found other friends, notably Celio Secondo Curione, the Italian Protestant refugee who taught rhetoric and enjoyed a great reputation as a humanist scholar.[13]

The peaceful situation was not to last very long. On October 27, 1553, Michael Servetus was burnt at the stake in Geneva. A large number of religious refugees who lived in exile in the Protestant cantons of the Swiss confederation had followed the trial of the Spanish heretic with growing uneasiness. Now that it had resulted in an execution which painfully recalled the methods of the Catholic Inquisition, a general feeling of disillusionment and insecurity spread among these people. Their common misgivings were very aptly expressed by a Swiss politician. In a letter to Calvin, Nikolaus Zurkinden, the highly respected town clerk of Bern, called the execution of Servetus a fatal and extremely dangerous mistake.[14] A few months later, Calvin published his famous *Defensio orthodoxae fidei*, an apology for the killing of heretics which was to defend and justify the measures taken against the Spaniard.[15]

In March 1554 appeared the little book which soon became and still is the main reason for Castellio's fame in history: *De haereticis an sint persequendi*.[16] It was not designed as a direct response to Calvin's tract, but it revealed very clearly that the death of Servetus had created a general apprehension and uneasiness which was not to be calmed down by any kind of *Defensio orthodoxae fidei*.

The Servetus affair was not mentioned at all in the little volume. What the reader found was a collection of texts and quotations from numerous writings of ancient and contemporary authors, all of them in favor of religious toleration and against capital punishment as a means of dealing with heretics.

The editor calls himself Martinus Bellius. He opens the discussion with a lengthy introduction addressed to Duke Christopher of Württemberg. Then he presents four extensive passages from writings of Luther, Johannes Brenz, Erasmus of Rotterdam, and Sebastian Franck. After this, there are a number of quotations from the works of the church fathers Augustine, Lactantius, Jerome, and John Chrysostomus. Among the contemporary witnesses we find Urbanus Rhegius, Otto Brunfels, Conrad Pellican, and Celio Secondo Curione. Somewhat surprisingly, even Calvin himself appears with two brief quotations defending the principle of religious toleration. Castellio is represented (under his own name) with a long passage from the preface to the Latin Bible of 1551, addressed to King Edward VI of England. At the end of the collection there are two lengthy tracts whose authors call themselves Georgius Kleinbergius and Basilius Montfortius respectively.

Sometime after the Latin edition of the *De haereticis* there appeared a French translation. This second edition contained an additional preface addressed to another Protestant prince of Germany, namely Count William of Hesse. Apart from this, the reader finds a second quotation from Luther and a number of supplementary texts from the writings of minor German reformers.[17]

The book at once created a great deal of sensation and indignation, especially in Geneva and Zürich. Everyone started wondering who the compiler of the publication was and who had initiated the enterprise.

When he read the book in late March 1554, Theodore Beza, who at that time still lived and taught in Lausanne, at once recognized in the introductory essay of Martin Bellius the same spirit that he had found in the dedicatory epistle of Castellio's Latin Bible. This led him to the assumption that "Martinus Bellius" was only a pseudonym, and that the Savoyard who had once been Calvin's trusted collaborator was the real author of the address to Duke Christopher of Württemberg. Beza concluded that Castellio had been the editor of the *De haereticis* and that he had been assisted by some of his refugee friends like Lelio Sozzini and Celio Secondo Curione. Although the title-page of the Latin edition indicated that it had been printed at Magdeburg, Beza soon realized that the book had been printed in Basel. "I am pretty sure", he wrote to Heinrich Bullinger, "that this Magdeburg is situated on the Rhine."[18] But who were Georgius Kleinberg and Basilius Montfort? Did not these names, like that of Martinus Bellius, remind one of Châteillon or Castellio? The reader familiar with German, French and Latin could not doubt their similarity. Theodore Beza was right in his assumption. The identity of Castellio, Bellius and Montfort has been established several times since. It is generally considered very likely that Castellio also wrote the piece of Georgius Kleinberg.[19] The Latin edition of the *De haereticis* has been proved to be a product of the press of Oporinus.[20]

The reaction from Geneva was not slow in coming. Already in August 1554, Beza published a refutation *De haereticis a civili magistratu puniendis*.[21] With this, the battle was on. It was to be fought with increasing sharpness and passion until Castellio's death. Several times, the Savoyard scholar had to take up his pen and defend himself against the attacks from Geneva which often culminated in personal abuse and insult. Castellio's defense, although less personal, was no less sharp. If we compare the pamphlets of Calvin and Beza with Castellio's answers we notice a certain similarity of style and tone which reminds us that all three authors came from the same intellectual and educational background, namely that of French literary humanism.[22] It is impossible here to give full bibliographical information on these writings. We must, however, point to the fact that, whereas the Genevan pamphlets were all printed and therefore widely propagated, most of Castellio's answers were only circulated in manuscript because the Basel authorities did not permit them to be printed. Thus, Castellio's tract *Contra libellum Calvini* which was intended to refute Calvin's *Defensio orthodoxae*

fidei and which contained a detailed discussion of the Servetus affair, remained unpublished until 1612 when it was printed in
Holland.[23] When the Basel bookprinter Pietro Perna published
Castellio's *Dialogi quatuor* and some other tracts in 1578, fifteen
years after the author's death, he was fined and jailed for having
evaded the censors.[24]

The long controversy between Castellio and the Genevan reformers did not revolve around the sole question of how to deal with heretics. It also touched upon the doctrines of predestination, election,
and original sin which the Savoyard humanist criticized on several
occasions. Furthermore, Castellio was savagely attacked as a translator of the Bible. Both Calvin and Beza repeatedly charged him
with blasphemy for having turned the Holy Scriptures into the language of the pagan Cicero and into that of the lowly French peasants. They completely failed to understand Castellio's pedagogical
intentions.[25]

Apart from the Genevan attacks, Castellio was also criticized
heavily by some theologians of Basel. His situation became particularly dangerous in 1559 when it was discovered that he had maintained personal relations with David Joris, the Dutch Anabaptist
leader who had lived in Basel under the assumed name of Jan van
Brugge.[26]

To the modern student of Castellio's life it is astonishing that, in
spite of these tribulations, Castellio was able to remain productive as
a teacher and classical scholar. Many foreign students attended his
classes. They came from the Netherlands, Germany, Poland,
France, and Italy. His scholarly publications were amazingly
numerous. In 1557 he published a Latin translation of the *German
Theology*. The Latin Bible was revised several times during the 50s.
The same applied to the *Dialogi sacri*. Both of these works were to
remain popular in Protestant Europe down to the end of the eighteenth century. Castellio also published editions of classical authors
including the works of Xenophon, Herodotus, Diodorus, Thucy-
dides, and Homer. In 1562 he wrote a little book on religious toleration which stood outside the controversy with the Genevans. Under
the title *Conseil à la France désolée* it dealt with the origins and motives of the French religious wars. Shortly before his death he
brought out an edition of the *Imitation of Christ*.[27] The most important work of his last years, however, was the long essay *De arte
dubitandi*, a book which appears to the modern reader like a bridge
between sixteenth century Christian Humanism and the beginnings

of Rationalism. With the exception of one chapter it was never published until 1937.[28]

It is quite evident that Castellio's idea of religious toleration was based entirely on the Holy Scriptures. The Bible was the book to whose study he devoted most of his time and energy. Many reformers have translated it in full or in part. Castellio, it must be repeated here, had given the world *two* translations of the entire Bible. In his opinion, the propagation of the Word of God as revealed in Scriptures was deeply and closely related to the propagation of tolerance. This becomes quite clear when we take a look at the preface to his Latin Bible translation of 1551.

Within the general development of Castellio's philosophical and theological thought, this dedicatory epistle to King Edward VI of England occupies a place of particular interest. It is the earliest of his writings in which the plea for religious toleration is put forth. The fact that it was written and published in the first months of 1551 shows very clearly that this plea was not precipitated by the execution of Servetus, but that it had begun to take shape in Castellio's mind already several years earlier. It can safely be assumed that Castellio's ideas were more widely propagated through this preface than through the *De haereticis* and the later pamphlets against Calvin and Bèza, because the Latin Bible was republished more often than these works. The preface of 1551 does not yet bear the marks of the struggle which were to characterize many of Castellio's later writings. It still lacks their passionate tone and their rhetorical power. Castellio does not yet speak as an accuser. He avoids direct allusions to persons and events. Only here and there does the reader perceive traces of the author's personal experience with the intolerance he endured from the pastors of Geneva before he decided to leave that city in 1544.

In spite of its dispassionate tone and somewhat theoretical method of argumentation, the epistle to the youthful King of England reveals the characteristic elements of Castellio's thought clearly and comprehensively.[29]

At the outset Castellio indicates the motive behind his Latin translation of the Holy Scriptures. He undertakes the arduous task in order to make known the Word of God among all nations. He wants to lay it before the reader in the clearest, most perspicuous, and most elegant of languages: in that of Cicero. But the humanist has no illusions. Learned translations alone will not bring the Word of God toward its fulfilment. In spite of a general interest in arts and letters the world dwells in a state of darkest ignorance concerning many religious matters. This ignorance becomes obvious again and again in all the innumerable conflicts which arise between Christians who do not agree over the meaning of certain passages of the Bible. The reason for the many misunderstandings, Castellio asserts, is not indifference toward God's commandments, but rather a general lack of real Christian piety and charity. Only when these virtues are practiced again will fatal ignorance be lifted from the world. Only then will the "golden century" begin of which the prophet speaks when he predicts the coming of an age of peace in which the peoples "shall beat their swords into plowshares and their spears into pruning hooks." This age is still far away, and the signs of its coming are scarce.

After reading these sentences one recalls that the humanist who wrote them was also to translate and re-edit the *German Theology* and the *Imitation of Christ*.[30] The ethical basis and the spiritualistic tendencies that seem to have characterized his theological ideas even before the outbreak of the conflict with Calvin and Beza are also discernible in another paragraph of the preface to Edward VI. Here Castellio comes back to an analysis of the basic evils of his time. It is not at all surprising that he was to include this passage in the *De haereticis*.[31] It leads straight to the center of his plea for toleration, and may well deserve to be summarized here, too. Castellio points out that many Christians who do not agree with each other on how to fulfill certain commandments of God resort to violence and go as far as to kill each other. They do not imitate the many examples of human and divine clemency set before them in the Holy Scriptures, and when they persecute and kill others who hold different opinions they pretend to act in the name of God. They disregard the parable of the tares, and they repeatedly forget that Christ admonished his followers: "Judge not that you be not judged." The use of terrestrial arms in conflicts over spiritual things is absurd. Only the true arms of the Christian religion will lead to peace and understanding and to the victory of truth. They are learning, patience, modesty, diligence, clemency, sincerity, devotion—an interesting, indeed one is tempted to say a truly humanist catalogue of Christian virtues! And here Castellio proceeds to a definition of the authority of the Christian magistrate. It is strictly limited to the punishment of those who commit crimes like murder, adultery, theft, false witness, and the like, "which God has commanded to be punished." The civil magistrate "who is ordained of God for the defense of the good" ("*a*

Deo ad bonos defendendos constitutus") has to preserve peace and order. He has no right to interfere with the religious affairs of the subjects. Over these only God has the power to judge; his children have to wait in all humility until his judgement is given. Those who try to anticipate it and permit themselves to persecute or even kill others on account of religious disagreement do not act in his name. On the contrary: they commit the worst of sins against his commandment.[32]

Here we have Castellio's plea for religious toleration in the Christian state set forth with clear-cut brevity. Taken in this form and used as the basis of a general appreciation of Castellio's thought it might, however, lead to over-simplifications that would place the Savoyard humanist too far out on the so-called "left wing of the Reformation." When we turn our attention to the *De haereticis*, we realize that Castellio was able to see the whole problem in a broader context and to analyze it with greater discrimination. It is quite natural that all the arguments put forth in the preface of the Latin Bible should be stated here again, but the more systematic method and wider scope of the book lead to the discussion of some new ones. As we have seen, the *De haereticis* consists of a collection of documents and of a number of contributions from Castellio's own pen, the most important being the preface of Martinus Bellius.

Here the humanist shows very clearly that the problem of religious toleration is in fact a combination of two problems. One is the question of the relationship between the temporal and the spiritual authorities in religious matters. The other is the eternal difficulty in recognizing the true heretic. Castellio does not deny the validity of the term. In the preface of Martinus Bellius he defines the heretic as one who does not agree with the "essentials" of the Christian religion. There *are* heretics, he asserts, and he admits that he does not like them. If he recommends that they be treated with clemency, it is because he sees two great dangers here: "The first is that he be held for a heretic, who is not a heretic . . . The other danger is that he who is really a heretic be punished more severely or in a manner other that that required by Christian discipline."[33]

When he comes to the question of how the temporal magistrate of the Christian state ought to deal with heretics, Castellio appears somewhat more conservative than in the preface to the Latin Bible. He grants that the magistrate must preserve peace and order. If there are heretics who disturb the public peace, the magistrate may punish them with fines or even with banishment. Capital punishment must, however, always be excluded.[34] No human being can ever maintain with certainty that another human being is a heretic. If it is done, there is always the great danger that innocent people may be put to death. This is the reason why it can never be permitted to kill a man in order to further the propagation of a religious doctrine. This opinion was to be set forth most impressively in Castellio's pamphlet *Contra libellum Calvini* where we find the sentence: "To kill a man is not to defend a doctrine; it is to kill a man."[35]

Castellio does not want to leave the heretic to himself, however. He wants to meet him in the spirit of Christian charity and bring him back to the way of truth. This, he asserts, cannot be done through violence but only through brotherly love and through the shining example of a true imitation of Christ.[36]

Thus, the Savoyard humanist stands far apart from religious relativism or indifference. It does not surprise us to see that particularly the French rationalists like Pierre Bayle and Voltaire, although they professed a certain admiration for Castellio, did not understand the full significance of his irenic ideas.[37]

We have said that Castellio's concept of toleration is based upon the Holy Scriptures and that it is closely related to his general theological thought. This becomes obvious when we try to recognize the historical background of his intellectual achievements. In order to do this we have to glance again through the pages of the *De haereticis*, and we can easily perceive which of the witnesses quoted here are closest to the ideas expressed by Martinus Bellius, George Kleinberg, and Basilius Montfort: they are Erasmus of Rotterdam and Sebastian Franck.

Castellio had already become acquainted with the works of the Dutch humanist as a student. The texts of Erasmus in the *De haereticis* are from the well-known controversies with Noël Beda and the Spanish monks.[38] In Conrad Pellican's contribution we find another passage from one of Erasmus' works, namely from his commentary on the parable of the tares.[39] Castellio's knowledge of the writings of Erasmus may well have been furthered by Bonifacius Amerbach who was the custodian of the correspondences and other papers which his great friend had left behind.

There are several traits in Castellio's intellectual personality which point to a possible influence of the writings of Erasmus: We think for instance of his interest in late medieval spiritualism which led him to undertake new editions of the *German Theology* and the

Imitation of Christ. In addition to this we must point to his constant
emphasis on practical piety, to his rejection of "non-essentials" in
the teaching of the Holy Scriptures and finally to his outspoken scep-
ticism toward dogmatic systems and denominational organizations.
A similar congeniality exists between Castellio and Sebastian
Franck. The wandering scholar from Donauwörth who did not
want to be identified with any religious group or organization had
died in Basel three years before Castellio arrived there. In his remarkable *Chronica, Zeytbuch und Geschichtsbibel* (1531, 1536)
Franck had already assembled much of the material Castellio was to
use in the *De haereticis*. It is to be found in the third part of the work
in a long chapter whose title is *Chronicle of the Roman heretics*.
Here Franck had quoted the same passages from Chrysostomus,
Augustine, Jerome, and also the texts from the writings of Erasmus,
Luther, and Brenz that were to appear again in Castellio's antholo-
gy. It cannot be doubted that Sebastian Franck's *Chronicle* was one
of the main sources of the *De haereticis*.[40] The assertion of the German humanist that those who suffered persecution as heretics were
often better Christians than those who persecuted and killed them,
is often repeated in Castellio's writings. In the *De haereticis* Franck
appears with a passage from his *Chronicle* in which he discusses the
question of whether it is possible to recognize the true heretic. His
answer is practically the same as that given by Castellio in the preface to the Latin Bible and in the address of Martinus Bellius to Duke
Christopher of Württemberg: only God himself recognizes the true
heretic and has the authority to punish him. Because men have always anticipated His judgment, there have always been persecutions. The frightening thing, according to Franck, is that these persecutions are still going on and that there does not seem to be an end
to them.

Among Castellio's intellectual predecessors we must not overlook
the late medieval bishop and cardinal Nicholas of Cusa. It cannot be
denied that this uniquely original thinker had arrived at his plea for
religious toleration from very different presuppositions, but the plea
itself was practically the same. Like Castellio, Nicholas of Cusa
clearly saw the difference between true Christian toleration and rel-
ativistic indifference. How well Castellio knew the writings of Nicholas is difficult to tell. Their first complete edition was published in
Basel in 1565, two years after the humanist's death.[41]

To what extent was Castellio, compared with his intellectual forerunners, an independent theological thinker? As far as his general

theological conceptions are concerned, he was not very original, but he was original in the way he applied these conceptions to the practical needs of his time. As a social critic we can compare him with Erasmus. There is one important difference, however. To the Dutch humanist biblical revelation and ecclesiastical tradition always remained the starting point of theological reflection. Castellio's own *"liberum arbitrium"* was founded rather upon human reason. Nowhere in his writings is this more obvious than in the second part of the *De arte dubitandi* where he summarizes his doctrinal views. Here we find a number of critical remarks on the doctrine of the trinity, formulated as questions rather than as definite statements.[42] We also find his definition of justification which he saw as a subjective reconciliation between man and God, free from any prescribed form of penitence. He held that many scriptural truths and teachings are above human reason but that none is against it. From here he developed his view that all religious questions, including that of how to deal with heretics, could and would eventually be solved by man who had been given the power of reason by his Creator.[43]

Like Cusanus and Erasmus, Castellio argued for toleration on the basis of his hope for eventual reconciliation, that is, for the restoration of religious consensus within the whole of Christendom. This argument is typical of the humanist way of thinking. More pragmatic arguments in favor of toleration can be found in the later sixteenth century. One of them is what I would like to call the political argument: toleration is defended in view, not of an eventual reconciliation, but of a permanent co-existence of different religions within the same state. The main purpose is no longer the establishment or re-establishment of religious unity, but the preservation of the political order. This argument was brought forth by various French authors at the beginning and towards the end of the religious wars. We can find it in the anonymous but nevertheless very famous *Exhortation aux princes et seigneurs du Conseil privé du Roy* of 1561, in some speeches of the chancellor Michel de L'Hospital after the failure of the colloque of Poissy, and we can also find it in several writings of the "Politiques" who became influential as a party of mediation in the 1570s. Castellio himself took it up in his *Conseil à la France désolée* of 1562 in which he said that two churches ought to be tolerated in France so that the monarchy could be saved. He also pointed to the *Exhortation*, praised it highly and declared that everyone in France ought to read it, Catholics as well as Protestants. This shows us that the Savoyard humanist was versatile enough to argue quite pragmatically when it was required, and that he had a very clear notion about what was needed to restore peace in France.[44]

In most textbooks on the age of the Reformation, Castellio is discussed among the Protestant radicals. This is quite understandable, particularly in view of his later works such as the *De arte dubitandi* which in many passages seem indeed to point toward the beginnings of rationalism. On the other hand we must not overlook the conservative elements of Castellio's intellectual personality. An important example is his view of the office of Christian princes and magistrates. He never doubted the divine character of this office. Although he believed that there was a limit to the authority of the civil magistrate in religious matters, he never advocated the separation of Church and State. On the contrary, he was convinced that the State carried a great spiritual responsibility as the protector of the fundamentals of true Christian religion which were faith in God, obedience to His Word, peace, brotherly love, and mutual understanding among the subjects. Castellio believed that the men who govern Christian states, must make it possible for every one of their subjects to follow Christ and to live *"sancte, juste, et pie."*[45]

The history of Castellio's posthumous influence is an interesting but difficult topic. We can observe his influence most easily wherever we find posthumous translations and re-editions of his writings, but we must also remember that many of Castellio's highly controversial tracts were often re-printed anonymously or circulated in manuscript for a long time. Not a few later thinkers who read them and used them for their own theological, philosophical, or political treatises, did not bother or dare to mention the name of their author. If Castellio was often praised by people who agreed with his views, he was even more often condemned as one of the worst heretics of his time by orthodox Calvinists, Lutherans and Roman Catholics alike. As long as denominational controversies continued to dominate intellectual and political life in Europe it was not always a wise thing to quote Castellio as an authority or to indicate open agreement with his views. Many seventeenth- and eighteenth-century writings on religious toleration seem to reflect the influence of Castellio, but it is frequently impossible to prove that the authors were acquainted with his works. In such cases we must be careful not to make hasty conjectures, but rather to allow for indirect influence through one or more intermediate authorities.

In our attempt to survey the influence of Castellio's ideas upon later authors or intellectual movements, we shall be as brief as possible. Nowhere in sixteenth- and seventeenth-century Europe did the ideas and writings of the Savoyard humanist bring about more directly visible effects than in the Netherlands. Already in his lifetime Castellio had been well-known to many humanist scholars of that country. A number of them had been among his students at Basel. Others corresponded with him though they had never met him personally. Among these people one must seek the first readers and propagators of his writings. Dutch Calvinist authors in the late sixteenth century often made derogatory remarks about the "Castellionists" or "Bellianists" who agreed with the heresies of the Savoyard. These "Bellianists" were, however, not a clearly recognizable movement. They could be found among the Mennonites and among the adherents of the "Family of Love," but also in Reformed, Lutheran, and even Roman Catholic circles.

Dutch translations and re-editions of Castellio's works began to appear shortly after the humanist's death. From around 1580 we can observe a gradual increase in their number and, along with this, a growing criticism of Castellio's views in Calvinist literature. The greatest number of Dutch editions of Castellio's writings was produced during the first two decades of the seventeenth century at the time of the Arminian and Remonstrant controversies. The Remonstrants who were to be banished by the Synod of Dordrecht obviously considered Castellio one of their most significant forerunners. After 1618 the new editions of his writings became less frequent. But his fame remained alive especially among the members of the Remonstrant brotherhood which had been re-admitted to the Dutch Republic in 1626.[46]

Castellio's writings and ideas were also popular within the Antitrinitarian Churches of Poland and Transylvania. Fausto Sozzini had met the humanist in his youth. When he returned to Basel in the 1570s he studied the papers Castellio had left to some of his friends. As we have mentioned above, a number of these manuscripts were published in 1578 under the title *Dialogi quatuor*. For this publication Sozzini wrote a preface full of praise and enthusiasm. When he moved to Eastern Europe—first to Transylvania and then to Poland—he took some copies of the book with him.[47] Although Castellio's works were frequently quoted by Polish Socinians of the late sixteenth and early seventeenth century, no re-editions were produced. We know of only one Polish translation of any writing of the Savoyard humanist. Characteristically, it is one of the tracts published in Basel in 1578, namely the dialogue "*De fide.*" The name of the translator is unknown. His work was never published and has been discovered as a manuscript only a few years ago.[48] Among the Antitrinitarians of Transylvania Castellio was equally well known. In the second half of the sixteenth century one of their leading scholars, the one-time Dominican Jacob Paleologus, wrote a lengthy apology of Castellio which he addressed to Theodore Beza. This tract has also been preserved in manuscript only.[49]

Several of Castellio's writings were re-edited in England. Some of them caused minor controversies during the reign of Queen Elizabeth. In the seventeenth century a number of English translations appeared. When John Locke lived in Dutch exile he must have become acquainted with most of Castellio's printed works. He took a number of them back to England and kept them in his library. In 1693 he discussed the possibility of publishing a complete edition of the humanist's writings with his Dutch friend Philip van Limborch, a leading Remonstrant historian. Unfortunately, the plan was never realized. There is, finally, some evidence that Castellio's ideas were also known to some of the early English Antitrinitarians of the seventeenth century.[50]

On the whole, the influence of Castellio's writings on the intellectual development of England was mainly indirect. This applies even more to the propagation of his ideas on the North American continent. His concept of religious toleration would certainly not have found much support among the New England Puritans. It would have appealed much more to the Mennonites, Schwenckfelders, Quakers, and other spiritualistic minorities. Roger Williams, too, might have understood and appreciated its implications. Although his writings contain passages which seem to reflect the influence of Castellio, we have no evidence that he knew the *De haereticis*, let alone the other writings concerning religious toleration.[51]

From the middle of the eighteenth to the middle of the nineteenth century, the works and ideas of Sebastian Castellio were largely forgotten. A general revival of interest was brought about by French scholars in the 1880s and 1890s.[52] A number of very valuable contributions toward a better understanding of Castellio's historical significance have since been made by American authors.[53]

To the modern student of the Reformation, Castellio is one of those figures who do not lend themselves easily to an identification with one particular movement or intellectual current of the period.

Like Sebastian Franck, Hans Denck, Schwenckfeld, or even Erasmus himself, Castellio is one of the great individualists of his age. He was a lonely man among his contemporaries in Basel and elsewhere. He was misunderstood, abused, and insulted in many ways, Although he could and did fight back with a pen no less sharp than those of his adversaries, his life was a continuous struggle. Out of it came the passionate plea for religious freedom, liberty of conscience, and openmindedness toward the fellow man who is of different faith. Castellio's voice surely deserves to be heard in our time as well. It deserves to be heard by all those who like to call our present age the ecumenical era.

Conclusion

Looking back over the different aspects of the Basel city republic in the sixteenth century that have been discussed here, we may well ask ourselves which of them might be called the most characteristic or significant. In reply I would venture to point to the continuity of the humanist ideals of knowledge. These ideals had taken shape before the Reformation. They had not been destroyed by the religious renewal, and they continued to flourish among the educated groups of the population for a long time afterwards. Basel remained attractive to prominent and lowly visitors from all over Europe even after Calvinist orthodoxy had won its victory in 1585.

It is no exaggeration to say that some of the intellectual impulses that originated in the humanist circles of sixteenth-century Basel reached a general historical relevance which can be compared with those of the Reformation itself. One may think of the scholarly achievements of Erasmus and his contemporaries and of Castellio's concept of religious toleration, but one should not overlook the universalist and rationalist ideas of such men as Curione and Fausto Sozzini. Neither should the scientific tradition of Paracelsus be forgotten. It found some of its most ardent students and advocates in the circle of scholars around Pietro Perna and Theodore Zwinger. Finally, we must always remember that most of the books and tracts written by these men were written from a standpoint in opposition to the Reformed state church.

The ecclesiastical and political leaders of the "Basilea reformata" certainly did not practice absolute toleration vis-à-vis their humanist critics. Leniency usually had its practical reasons. Some of the radical thinkers and writers were repeatedly harassed in all sorts of ways, and more than one of them experienced moments of despair during which he made plans to leave the city. Some of them actually did so.

The sixteenth-century city republic of Basel had no laws guaranteeing the peaceful coexistence of different religious beliefs. On the other hand there occurred no open religious persecution in Basel after the early 1530s. The followers of David Joris were punished

Conclusion

with relative gentleness in 1559. Some "heretics"—this must be admitted—died or left before the authorities could have taken hostile action against them. Without idealizing the general situation we can say, however, that from around 1500 through the mid-1520s, and then again from the early 1530s until the early 1580s the intellectual atmosphere of Basel was relatively open-minded. A considerable diversity of opinions and beliefs was possible. There is no doubt that this open-mindedness was the main reason of the fact that the "Basilea reformata" could become and remain a focal point of European late Renaissance culture for so long.

Still, we, must remember Stanisław Kot's statement that I quoted in the preface: Sixteenth-century Basel was not as important as Rome, Wittenberg, Geneva, and Paris. There is, I believe, still no reason to contradict this opinion, but we can observe—and I hope to have made this reasonably clear—that in the city republic of Basel there prevailed a relatively extensive intellectual freedom which favored the growth and the propagation of new ideas, some of which pointed far into the future. No such intellectual freedom prevailed in any of the afore-mentioned capitals of Europe.

Bibliographical Note

I have tried to make the notes accompanying each chapter as informative as possible so that a topical bibliography would not be necessary. A complete list of source editions and secondary works would take up too much space, and it would do no more than repeat information already given in the footnotes. Readers interested in special topics can easily find additional information in the very comprehensive and reliable *Basler Bibliographie* which is published regularly as a supplement to the *Basler Zeitschrift für Geschichte und Altertumskunde* (1902ff). Among recent monographs providing especially copious bibliographical information on sixteenth-century Basel, I would like to mention the books of Uwe Plath, *Calvin und Basel in den Jahren 1552–1556* (1974) and Hans Füglister, *Handwerksregiment* (1981).

Students who want to go beyond printed works will consult the records held in the "Staatsarchiv Basel-Stadt" and in the manuscript department of the Basel University Library. They will be pleased to discover that both repositories are very rich and well organized. The "Staatsarchiv" mainly holds the public records of the city's political, religious, social, and economic life, including the documents relating to the history of the University. The University Library, on the other hand, possesses a great number of personal writings, papers, and letters. The source editions are generally of very high quality, but most of them cover only the first half of the sixteenth century. The *Aktensammlung zur Geschichte der Basler Reformation*, edited by E. Dürr and P. Roth (6 vols., 1921–50) is one of the most comprehensive collections of its kind. It is most reliable for the late 1520s. Important documents are also included in volumes 9 and 10 of the *Urkundenbuch der Stadt Basel*, edited by R. Thommen (1905, 1908). Both works are supplemented by the series *Basler Chroniken* which was started in 1872, but which also contains such recent additions relating to the sixteenth century as the Travelbook of Thomas Platter the Younger (vol. 9, 1968) and Felix Platter's Diary (vol. 10, 1976). The *Amerbachkorrespondenz*, currently edited by Beat R. Jenny, has reached the year 1552 (vol. 8, 1974). Of fundamental importance for the history of the Reformation is Ernst Staehelin's edition of the *Briefe und Akten zum Leben Oekolampads* (2 vols., 1927, 1934). Whoever works on sixteenth-century Basel will always be grateful for the abundance of biographical information provided by volumes 1 and 2 of the *Matrikel der Universität Basel* (H.G. Wackernagel, ed., 1951, 1956).

The secondary literature on the history of Basel written and published since the early 19th century is very extensive. Some of the older works are still useful, notably Peter Ochs' *Geschichte der Stadt und Landschaft Basel* (8 volumes, 1786–1822). It contains a considerable number of documents which are not preserved anywhere else. The sixteenth century is covered in volume 6. Quite indispensable also are Andreas Heusler's *Verfassungsgeschichte der Stadt Basel in Mittelalter* (1860) and Traugott Geering's *Handel und Industrie der Stadt Basel: Zunftwesen und Wirtschaftsgeschichte bis zum Ende des XVII. Jahrhunderts* (1886). Among more modern surveys Rudolf Wackernagel's *Geschichte der Stadt Basel* (3 vols. in 4, 1907–1924) stands out as the most distinguished achievement. The history of the city republic is treated from its beginning down to the Reformation. Within these chronological limits Wackernagel's work is very comprehensive. It is most carefully and competently documented, (the author was State Archivist from 1877 to 1917), and still makes good reading. For the *"histoire événementielle"* it is unsurpassed. There are several shorter accounts which also include the modern and contemporary periods of the city's history. None of them bears comparison with Wackernagel's work. The best short survey is Paul Burckhardt's one-volume *Geschichte der Stadt Basel* (1957[2]). The new *Basler Stadtgeschichte* (vol. 2, 1981) by M. Alioth, U. Barth, and D. Huber is extremely brief, but it contains several interesting tables and charts. For the "Landschaft" the collective *Geschichte der Landschaft Basel und des Kantons Basel-Landschaft* (2 vols., 1932) is still useful. In addition to the *Basler Zeitschrift für Geschichte und Altertumskunde* there are two other annual publications, namely the *Basler Neujahrsblatt* (1872 ff) and the *Basler Stadtbuch* (1960 ff; formerly *Basler Jahrbuch*, 1879ff, and *Basler Taschenbuch*, 1850ff). A great deal of information on sixteenth-century local history can be found in these publications, particularly in the older volumes.

Finally, two series of historical monographs (mostly doctoral dissertations) must be mentioned here: The *Quellen und Forschungen zur Basler Geschichte* (1966ff) are published by the "Staatsarchiv" and exclusively devoted to local topics. The series *Basler Beiträge zur Geschichtswissenschaft* (1938 ff) appears under the auspices of the Department of History ("Historisches Seminar") of the University of Basel. Its topical range is very wide, but it has always included monographs on local history. A considerable number of recent studies on sixteenth-century Basel that are mentioned in the footnotes of the preceding chapters have been published as volumes of the *Basler Beiträge* (e.g. H. Füglister, vol. 143; U. Plath, vol. 133; M. Steinmann, vol. 105, P. Bietenholz, vol. 73).

Footnotes

Abbreviations

ABR   *Aktensammlung zur Geschichte der Basler Reformation in den Jahren 1519 bis Anfang 1534*, ed. E. Dürr, P. Roth, 6 vols. (Basel, 1921–1950)

AK   *Die Amerbachkorrespondenz*, ed. A. Hartmann and B.R. Jenny, 8 vols. (Basel, 1942–1974)

Allen   P.S. Allen (ed.), *Opus epistolarum Des. Erasmi Roterodami*, 12 vols. (Oxford, 1906–1958)

ARG   *Archiv für Reformationsgeschichte*

BC   *Basler Chroniken* (Leipzig, Basel, 1872ff)

BHR   *Bibliothèque d'Humanisme et Renaissance*

BUB   *Urkundenbuch der Stadt Basel*, ed. R. Thommen, vols. 9, 10 (Basel, 1905, 1908)

BZ   *Basler Zeitschrift für Geschichte und Altertumskunde*

CR   *Corpus Reformatorum* (Berlin, 1834ff)

EA   *Eidgenössische Abschiede* (Luzern, 1839ff)

Oek.   *Briefe und Akten zum Leben Oekolampads*, ed. E. Staehelin, 2 vols. (Leipzig, 1927, 1934)

StAB   Staatsarchiv Basel-Stadt

WA.B Luther, Martin. *Kritische Gesamtausgabe, Briefwechsel* (Weimar, 1930ff)

Z   *Huldreich Zwinglis Sämtliche Werke* (Berlin, Leipzig, Zürich, 1905ff)

Preface

[1]Stanisław Kot, "Polen und Basel zur Zeit des Königs Sigismund August (1548–1572) und die Anfänge kritischen Denkens in Polen," in BZ 41 (1942), pp. 105–153, cf. 108.

[2]Under the title "Das reformierte Basel als geistiger Brennpunkt Europas im 16. Jahrhundert" a German version of chapter III appeared in: Hans R. Guggisberg & Peter Rotach (eds.), *Ecclesia semper reformanda, Vorträge zum Basler Reformationsjubiläum, 1529–1979* (Basel, 1980), pp. 50–75.

Chapter I

[1]Hektor Ammann, "Wie gross war die mittelalterliche Stadt?", in: *Studium Generale* 9 (1956), pp. 503–506; repr. in: *Die Stadt des Mittelalters*, vol. 1 (Darmstadt, 1969), pp. 408–415; id., "Die Bevölkerung von Stadt und Landschaft Basel am Ausgang des Mittelalters," in: BZ 49 (1950), pp. 25–52; Dietrich W.H. Schwarz, "Die Städte der Schweiz im 15. Jahrhundert," in: Wilhelm Rausch (ed.), *Die Stadt am Ausgang des Mittelalters* (Linz, 1974), pp. 45–59; cf. also Franz Ehrensperger, *Basels Stellung im internationalen Handelsverkehr des Spätmittelalters* (Basel, 1972), esp. p. 361ff.

²Andreas Heusler, *Verfassungsgeschichte der Stadt Basel im Mittelalter* (Basel, 1860), p. 311.

³Cf. *infra*, p. 44

⁴EA III, 2, p. 1291; Hans Nabholz, Paul Kläui (eds.), *Quellenbuch zur Verfassungsgeschichte der Schweizerischen Eidgenossenschaft und der Kantone* (Aarau, 1947), pp. 75–85, cf. p. 80 (art. 18).

⁵Edgar Bonjour, "Basel im Schweizerbund," in: Edgar Bonjour, Albert Bruckner, *Basel und die Eidgenossen, Geschichte ihrer Beziehungen: Zur Erinnerung an Basels Eintritt in den Schweizerbund, 1501* (Basel, 1951), pp. 147–379.

⁶Cf. Nabholz, Kläui, *o.c.*, p. 78; Albert Bruckner, "Basels Weg zum Schweizerbund," in: *Basel und die Eidgenossen*, pp. 13–143.

⁷Ernst Staehelin, "Bâle et l'Alsace," in: *L'Humanisme en Alsace*, Association Guillaume Budé, Congrès de Strasbourg, 1938 (Paris, 1939), pp. 30–41; Hans R. Guggisberg, "Strasbourg et Bâle dans la Réforme," in: G. Livet et al. (eds.), *Strasbourg au coeur religieux du XVIe siècle* (Strasbourg, 1977), pp. 333–340, cf. p. 335.

⁸Cf. Rudolf Wackernagel, *Geschichte der Stadt Basel*, vol. 3 (Basel, 1924), p. 301f; A. Heusler, *Verfassungsgeschichte*, p. 427ff.

⁹The most recent and comprehensive account of the history of the Basel guilds is by Gustaf A. Wanner, *Zunftkraft und Zunftstolz* (Basel, 1976). Cf. also Traugott Geering, *Handel und Industrie der Stadt Basel: Zunftwesen und Wirtschaftsgeschichte bis zum Ende des 17. Jahrhunderts* (Basel, 1886), esp. p. 43ff.

¹⁰Cf. *infra*, p. 22.

¹¹Cf. *Handbuch der Schweizer Geschichte*, vol. 1 (Zürich, 1972), p. 554; Martin Alioth et al., *Basler Stadtgeschichte*, vol. 2 (Basel, 1981), pp. 70–80; Hans Füglister, *Handwerksregiment: Untersuchungen und Materialien zur sozialen und politischen Struktur der Stadt Basel in der ersten Hälfte des 16. Jahrhunderts* (Basel, 1981), pp. 137–256. Cf. also Alfred Müller, "Die Ratsverfassung der Stadt Basel von 1521 bis 1798," in: BZ 53 (1954), pp. 5–98.

¹²These figures were drawn from the pertinent archival documents in StAB (Klosterarchive) by my doctoral student Klaus Fischer who is preparing a dissertation on the Basel clergy before and during the Reformation. He kindly permitted me to mention them here.

¹³R. Wackernagel, *Geschichte der Stadt Basel*, vol. 2² (Basel, 1916), p. 616ff; Albert Bruckner, "Das bischöfliche Basel," in: Eugen A. Meier (ed.), *Basel: Eine illustrierte Stadtgeschichte* (Basel, 1969), p. 37ff.

¹⁴StAB, Städt. Urk. 1658; repr. in: Edgar Bonjour, *Die Universität Basel von den Anfängen bis zur Gegenwart, 1460–1960* (Basel, 1971²), p. 35f; cf. Berthe Widmer (ed.), *Enea Silvio Piccolomini, Papst Pius II: Ausgewählte Texte . . .* (Basel, 1959), pp. 18ff, 142ff.

¹⁵E. Bonjour, *Die Universität Basel*, pp. 60ff, 70f.

¹⁶Hans Kälin, *Papier in Basel bis 1500* (Basel, 1974), p. 138ff.

¹⁷A. Bruckner, "Die bischöfliche Stadt," p. 41.

¹⁸R. Wackernagel, *o.c.*, vol. 2², p. 612f; vol. 3, pp. 133ff, 166ff.

¹⁹T. Geering, *o.c.*, pp. 323–336.

²⁰R. Wackernagel, *o.c.*, vol. 3, pp. 143ff; Guido Kisch, "Forschungen zur Geschichte des Humanismus in Basel," in: *Archiv für Kulturgeschichte* 40 (1958), pp. 194–221; H.R. Guggisberg, "Neue Forschungen zur Geschichte des Basler Humanismus," in: *Schweizer Monatshefte* 49 (Nov. 1969), pp. 769–775.

²¹E. Bonjour, *Die Universität Basel*, pp. 19–33, esp. p. 33.

²²Cf. Andreas Staehelin, "Das geistige Basel," in: E.A. Meier (ed.), *Basel: Eine illustrierte Stadtgeschichte*, p. 53.

²³R. Wackernagel, *o.c.*, vol. 2², p. 598f.

²⁴*Ibid.*, pp. 600–602.

[25]Allen, vol. 2, no. 364; *The Collected Works of Erasmus*, vol. 3 (Toronto and Buffalo, 1976), no. 391A, p. 244; Yvonne Charlier, *Erasme et l'amitié d'après sa correspondance* (Paris, 1977), pp. 173ff.

[26]Cf. Roland H. Bainton, *Erasmus of Christendom* (New York, 1969), p. 131.

[27]Y. Charlier, *o.c.*, p. 316.

[28]Cf. *infra*, p. 30.

[29]Hans R. Guggisberg, "Fierté locale et tendances d'identification chez les humanistes bâlois à l'époque caroline," in: *Charles-Quint, le Rhin et la France* (Strasbourg, 1973), pp. 208ff.

[30]AK 2, 455, no. 945. On December 26, 1523 Bonifacius Amerbach's sister Margarethe wrote to her brother herself and entreated him to come home. She was afraid that he wanted to marry a French girl and told him that this would not be a good idea. *Ibid.*, 453, no. 943.

Chapter II

[1]Cf. first of all Natalie Z. Davis' studies in: *Society and Culture in Early Modern France* (London, 1975) and particularly her recent article "The Sacred and the Body Social in Sixteenth-Century Lyon," in: *Past and Present* 90 (Febr. 1981), pp. 40–70; also Susan Reynolds, *An Introduction to the History of English Medieval Towns* (Oxford, 1977), p. 164ff.

[2]Cf. Hans-Christoph Rublack, "Forschungsbericht Stadt und Reformation," in: Bernd Moeller (ed.), *Stadt und Kirche im 16. Jahrhundert* (Gütersloh, 1978), pp. 9–26, esp. p. 12, n. 18.

[3]Leopold von Ranke, *Deutsche Geschichte im Zeitalter der Reformation*, book VI, ch. 5: "Reform in den niederdeutschen Städten," cf. H.-Chr. Rublack, *l.c.*, p. 11.

[4]Bernd Moeller, *Reichsstadt und Reformation* (Gütersloh, 1962); -id., *Imperial Cities and the Reformation. Three Essays*. Trans. H.C. Midelfort and Mark U. Edwards (Philadelphia, 1972).

[5]Cf. for instance Robert W. Scribner, "Civic Unity and the Reformation in Erfurt," in: *Past and Present* 66 (1975), pp. 28–60, but quite particularly Thomas A. Brady, Jr., *Ruling Class, Regime and Reformation at Strasbourg, 1520–1555* (Leiden, 1978).

[6]Paul Roth, *Die Reformation in Basel, I. Teil: Die Vorbereitungsjahre (1525–1528)*, Basler Neujahrsblatt 114 (Basel, 1936); *Die Durchführung der Reformation in Basel 1529–1530*, Basler Neujahrsblatt 121 (Basel, 1943), *Durchbruch und Festsetzung der Reformation in Basel* (Basel, 1942).

[7]Hans Füglister, *Handwerksregiment*.

[8]A survey of the Basel religious pamphlets is being prepared by Michael Malich.

[9]R. Wackernagel, *o.c.*, vol. 3, p. 170.

[10]Letter of Conrad Pellican to Luther, March 15, 1520, in: Ernst Staehelin (ed.), *Das Buch der Basler Reformation* (Basel, 1929), pp. 25f, 29f; WA.B 2, pp. 354–359.

[11]Caspar Hedio, Letters to Zwingli, November 1519 through June 1520, CR 94 (1911), no. 98ff, p. 213ff (Z 7, Briefwechsel, Bd. 1).

[12]BC 1, 384; 7, 271; ABR 1, 34, no. 90; AK 2, 388, no. 879 (Joh. Froben to Bonif. Amerbach, Juy 6, 1522).

[13]J.M. Stayer, "Reublin and Brötli: The Revolutionary Beginnings of Swiss Anabaptism," in: M. Lienhard (ed.), *The Origins and Characteristics of Anabaptism / Les débuts et les caractéristiques de l'anabaptisme* (The Hague, 1977), pp. 83–102.

[14]The most comprehensive biographical account is still in Ernst Staehelin, *Das theologische Lebenswerk Johannes Oekolampads* (Leipzig, 1939). On Oecolampadius' relationship with Erasmus cf. E. Staehelin, "Erasmus und Oekolampad in ihrem Ringen um die Kirche Jesu Christi," in: *Gedenkschrift zum 400. Todestag des Erasmus von Rotterdam* (Basel, 1936), pp. 166–182.

[15]*Iudicium de doctore Martino Luthero; Paradoxon quod non sit onerosa Christianis confessio.* Printed in Zwickau and Augsburg respectively, cf. E. Staehelin, *o.c.*, p. 120ff.

[16]Oek. 1, p. 219f, no. 151; p. 254, no. 174; E. Staehelin, *Das theol. Lebenswerk Joh. Oekolampads*, p. 19o.

[17]Leonhard von Muralt, "Renaissance und Reformation," in: *Handbuch der Schweizer Geschichte*, vol. 1 (Zürich, 1972), p. 478.

[18]Cf. *Infra*, p. 29.

[19]ABR 1, p. 65ff, no. 151 (May/June 1523).

[20]Among the more interesting of these disputations was one concerning celibacy. It was held on February 16, 1524, on the initiative of Stephan Stör, minister of Liestal, who had married and then lost his post. ABR 1, p. 78, no. 170. The statements in favor of marriage were published in: *Von der Priester Ee, Disputation durch Stephanum Stör . . . gehalten* (Basel, 1524). In 1523 both the reform-minded preacher Wolfgang Wissenburg and Oecolampadius himself organized disputations. Nothing is known about their results, however. Cf. E. Staehelin, *Das Buch der Basler Reformation*, pp. 62, 65. In the spring of 1524, shortly after the Stör disputation, Guillaume Farel held a public debate in which he criticized the doctrine of good works and the conception of the mass as a good work. The success was so great that Farel ventured to hold public lectures. He assembled a small group of followers, French refugees like himself. After a few months, however, he was involved in many conflicts, and he quarreled also with Erasmus. This led to his banishment in July 1524. ABR 1, p, 95ff, no. 195; R. Wackernagel, *Geschichte der Stadt Basel*, vol. 3, p. 353. A disputation was announced by the City council on April 22, 1525, but it never took place, *ibid.*, p. 467.

[21]ABR 1, pp. 233, 263, 278, 368ff, 385ff (nos. 397, 413, 420, 471, 499); for the beginnings of Anabaptist propaganda, cf. ABR 2, pp. 33ff, nos. 46, 50.

[22]For a detailed account cf. P. Roth, *Die Reformation in Basel, I. Teil: Die Vorbereitungsjahre (1525-1528)*, pp. 5–24. Cf. BUB 10, p. 23ff, no. 34; p. 83ff, no. 72; p. 107ff, no. 95.

[23]Oek. 1, p. 413f, no. 298; CR 95, no. 404.

[24]*De genuina verborum Dei: hoc est corpus meum . . . expositione liber,* usually quoted as *Genuina expositio*. Cf. E. Staehelin, *Das theol. Lebenswerk Joh. Oekolampads*, p. 276ff.

[25]ABR 2, p. 715, no. 728 (September 23, 1527); *ibid.* 3, p. 50, no. 59 (February 27, 1528).

[26]ABR 3, p. 197ff, no. 291.

[27]P. Roth, *Durchbruch und Festsetzung der Reformation in Basel*, p. 26ff.

[28]ABR 3, pp. 383–409, no. 473.

[29]Rudolf Wackernagel, in his *Geschichte der Stadt Basel*, devoted a fundamental chapter to the year 1521; vol. 3, pp. 301–313.

[30]EA IV, 1a, pp. 1493–1498.

[31]H. Füglister, *Handwerksregiment*, p. 262ff; ABR 1, p. 30f, no. 81. The incident is known as the "Pensionensturm."

[32]StAB, Handel und Gewerbe Y 1, 1521, June 4; H. Füglister, *o.c.*, p. 276.

[33]T. Geering, *Handel und Industrie der Stadt Basel*, p. 373, StAB, Handel und Gewerbe Y 1, PP 10; Zunftakten B 3.

[34]There are a number of ms. copies of the "Gewerbeordnung" in the guild archives of the StAB. The most comprehensive copy is in Handel und Gewerbe Y 1. It is partly published in ABR 2, p. 191ff, no. 258.

[35]Paul Burckhardt, *Geschichte der Stadt Basel* (Basel, 1957²), pp. 10–13.

[36]H.R. Guggisberg, H. Füglister, "Die Basler Webernzunft als Trägerin reformatorischer Propaganda," in: Bernd Moeller (ed.), *Stadt und Kirche im 16. Jahrhundert* (Gütersloh, 1978), pp. 48–56.

[37]Ibid., pp. 51, 55.

[38]ABR 1, pp. 180–185, no. 316.

[39]H. Füglister, *Handwerksregiment*, p. 125ff.

[40]BC 7, p. 290; ABR 1, p. 328, no. 442.

[41]BC 1, p. 81f (The Chronicle of Fridolin Ryff); P. Roth, *Durchbruch und Festsetzung*, p. 27.

[42]The iconoclastic riot of February 9, 1529 is described in several contemporary Basel chronicles: BC 1, p. 447 ("Aufzeichnungen eines Basler Karthäusers"); BC 1, p. 86ff (Fridolin Ryff); BC 6, p. 116 (Konrad Schnitt). There is also a collection of testimonials in ABR 4, p. 70f, no. 80. Of particular interest is the account of what happened on February 8/9 in Oecolampadius' letter to Wolfgang Fabritius Capito of February 13, 1529, Oek. 2, p. 280ff, no. 636. The ferocity of the incident can at least in part be explained with the fact that February 8 and 9 were days of Carnival. Cf. Robert W. Scribner, "Reformation, Carnival and the World Turned Upside-Down," in: Ingrid Bátori (ed.), *Städtische Gesellschaft und Reformation* (Stuttgart, 1980), p. 239.

[43]BC 1, p. 88.

[44]ABR 3, p. 284ff, no. 387.

[45]ABR 3, p. 295ff, no. 398 (February 18, 1529).

[46]A. Heusler, *Verfassungsgeschichte*, p. 444; A. Müller, "Die Ratsverfassung der Stadt Basel," pp. 17, 20f.

[47]Oek. 2, p. 327, no. 664.

[48]"Oratio de reducenda excommunicatione," Oek. 2, p. 448ff, no. 750. E. Staehelin, *Das theol. Lebenswerk Joh. Oekolampads*, p. 507ff, 511.

[49]*Ibid.*, p. 519; ABR 5, p. 60ff, nos. 76, 77, 78.

[50]ABR 3, p. 383ff, no. 473; ABR 6, p 403, no. 400. Concerning the Basel Confession cf. Richard Stauffer, "Das Basler Bekenntnis von 1534," in: H.R. Guggisberg, P. Rotach (eds.), *Ecclesia semper reformanda, Vorträge zum Basler Reformationsjubiläum, 1529–1979* (Basel, 1980), pp. 28–49.

[51]Paul Burckhardt, *Die Basler Täufer, ein Beitrag zur schweizerischen Reformationsgeschichte* (Basel, 1898), p. 51ff; Hanspeter Jecker, "Die Basler Täufer: Studien zur Vor- und Frühgeschichte," in: BZ 80 (1980), pp. 5–131. On Oecolampadius and the persecution of the Anabaptists see E. Staehelin, *Das theol. Lebenswerk des Joh. Oekolampad*, p. 527ff.

[52]R. Wackernagel, *Geschichte der Stadt Basel*, vol. 3, p. 325f.

[53]Cf. Vadianische Briefsammlung, E. Arbenz, H. Wartmann (eds.), in: *Mitteilungen zur vaterländischen Geschichte* 28–30 (St. Gallen, 1902ff); E. Zellweger, "Der erste reformierte Pfarrer zu St. Leonhard in Basel . . . ," in: *Gottesreich und Menschenreich, Ernst Staehelin zum 80. Geburtstag*, ed. M. Geiger (Basel, 1969), pp. 89–102; Klaus Fischer, *Markus Bertschi und das reformierte Basel*, ms., Basel, 1975.

[54]H.G. Wackernagel (ed.), *Die Matrikel der Universität Basel*, vol. 2 (Basel, 1956), pp. 11, 62, 103.

[55]Cf. for instance Bernd Moeller's comparison between Basel and Lübeck as urban centers of the Reformation: "Die Basler Reformation in ihrem stadtgeschichtlichen Zusammenhang," in: *Ecclesia semper reformanda*, pp. 11–27.

[56]Thomas A. Brady, Jr., *Ruling Class, Regime and Reformation at Strasbourg*, p. 291ff.

Chapter III

[1]Cf. P. Burckhardt, *Geschichte der Stadt Basel*; M. Alioth et al., *Basler Stadtgeschichte*, vol. 2; E.A. Meier (ed.), *Basel: Eine illustrierte Stadtgeschichte*.

[2]Werner Kaegi, *Humanistische Kontinuität im konfessionellen Zeitalter*, Schriften der "Freunde der Universität Basel," Heft 8 (Basel, 1954).

[3]Kurt Maeder, *Die Via Media in der schweizerischen Reformation* (Zürich, 1970),

p. 125; Theophil Burckhardt-Biedermann, *Bonifacius Amerbach und die Reformation* (Basel, 1894).

[4]Max Geiger, *Die Basler Kirche und Theologie im Zeitalter der Hochorthodoxie* (Zollikon/Zürich, 1952), p. 15.

[5]BC 8 (Basel, 1945), pp. 155, 318ff; Paul Burckhardt, *Basel in den ersten Jahren nach der Reformation* (Basel, 1946), p. 53f.

[6]E. Bonjour, *Die Universität Basel*, p. 127.

[7]Roland H. Bainton, *David Joris, Wiedertäufer und Kämpfer für Toleranz im 16. Jahrhundert* (Leipzig, 1937), p. 157; Hanspeter Jecker, *Die Behandlung der "Fremden" in Basel*, ms., Basel, 1977, p. 6.

[8]Andreas Staehelin, "Die Refugiantenfamilien und die Entwicklung der baslerischen Wirtschaft," in: *Der Schweizer Familienforscher* 29 (1962), pp. 85–95; T. Geering, *Handel und Industrie der Stadt Basel*, p. 440ff.

[9]Quoted by Peter Ochs, *Geschichte der Stadt und Landschaft Basel*, vol. 6 (Basel, 1821), p. 491f.

[10]Franz Gschwind, *Bevölkerungsentwicklung und Wirtschaftsstruktur der Landschaft Basel im 18. Jahrhundert* (Liestal, 1977), p. 167f.

[11]H. Jecker, *l.c.*, Appendix, Table 4.

[12]F. Gschwind, *o.c.*, p. 140.

[13]A. Staehelin, *l.c.*, p. 87.

[14]Petrus Ramus, *Basilea, eine Rede an die Stadt Basel aus dem Jahre 1570*, transl. and introd. by Hans Fleig (Basel, 1944), p. 35. Cf. Peter G. Bietenholz, *Basle and France in the Sixteenth Century* (Geneva, 1971), p. 153ff.

[15]E. Bonjour, *Die Universität Basel*, p. 221; Marc Sieber, "Die Universität Basel im 16. Jahrhundert und ihre englischen Besucher," in: *BZ* 55 (1956), pp. 75–112; H.R. Guggisberg, "Die niederländischen Studenten an der Universität Basel von 1532 bis zum Ende des 17. Jahrhunderts," *ibid.*, 58/59 (1959), pp. 231–288; Eugénie Droz, "Les étudiants français de Bâle," *BHR* 20 (1958), pp. 108–141; Giovanni Busino, "Italiani all'università di Basilea dal 1460 al 1601," *ibid.*, 20 (1958), pp. 497–526.

[16]Cf. Frederic C. Church, *The Italian Reformers, 1534–1564* (New York, 1932), p. 273ff; Delio Cantimori, *Italienische Haeretiker der Spätrenaissance* (Basel, 1949), p. 85ff; M. Kutter, *Celio Secondo Curione, sein Leben und sein werk, 1503–1569* (Basel, 1955); Ferdinand Buissan, *Sébastien Castellion, sa vie et son oeuvre*, 2 vols. (Paris, 1892), vol. 1, p. 335ff.

[17]Cf. *infra*, p. 61.

[18]W. Kaegi, *Humanistische Kontinuität*, p. 12; cf. Peter Bietenholz, *Der italienische Humanismus und die Blütezeit des Buchdrucks in Basel* (Basel und Stuttgart, 1959). This study is a sequel to the older book by Friedrich Luchsinger, *Der Basler Buchdruck als Vermittler italienischen Geistes, 1470–1529* (Basel, 1953). It does not surprise us to observe that after 1530 young Basel scholars resumed the old tradition of improving their education with extended trips through Italy; Verena Vetter, *Baslerische Italienreisen vom ausgehenden Mittelalter bis in das 17. Jahrhundert* (Basel, 1952), p. 48ff.

[19]Martin Steinmann, *Johannes Oporinus, ein Basler Buchdrucker um die Mitte des 16. Jahrhunderts* (Basel und Stuttgart, 1967), p. 20ff.

[20]Antonio Rotondò, "Pietro Perna e la vita culturale e religiosa di Basilea fra il 1570 e il 1580," in: Id (ed.), *Studi e Ricerche di storia ereticale del Cinquecento*, vol. 1 (Turin, 1974), pp. 273–394; Leandro Perini, "Note e documenti su Pietro Perna . . . ," in: *Nuova rivista storica* 50 (1966), pp. 145–200; id., "Ancora sul libraiotipografo P.P.," *ibid.* 51 (1967), pp. 366–404; M. Welti, "Le grand amateur de la Renaissance tardive à Bâle: Pierre Perna éditeur, imprimeur et libraire," in: *L'Humanisme allemand (1480–1540)* (Paris, 1979), pp. 131–138.

[21]Werner Kaegi, "Machiavelli in Basel," in *Historische Meditationen* (Zürich, 1942), pp. 119–181, esp. 133ff.

[22]H.R. Guggisberg, "Pietro Perna, Fausto Sozzini und die Dialogi quatuor Sebastian

Castellios," in: *Studia bibliographica in honorem H. de la Fontaine Verwey* (Amsterdam, 1968), pp. 173–201.

[23]M. Steinmann, *o.c.*, p. 35.

[24]Carlos Gilly, "Zwischen Erfahrung und Spekulation: Theodor Zwinger und die religiöse und kulturelle Krise seiner Zeit," in: BZ 77 (1977), pp. 57–137, esp. p. 90ff; id. "Zwischen Erfahrung und Spekulation . . . , 2. Teil," *ibid.* 79 (1979), pp. 125–223.

[25]H.R. Guggisberg, "Pietro Perna," p. 192ff.

[26]". . . der tüfel hett uns mitt dem nüwen Bapsttumb beschissen." Cf. M. Steinmann, *o.c.*, p. 110.

[27]Rudolf Thommen, "Zensur und Universität in Basel bis 1799," in: *Basler Jahrbuch 1944* (Basel, 1944), pp. 49–82; M. Steinmann, *o.c.*, pp. 22ff, 94: According to the regulations of 1524 the censorship committee consisted of the non-acting mayor ("Altbürgermeister"), the superior guild master ("Oberst Zunftmeister"), and the town clerk ("Stadtschreiber"). These officials had so many other duties that they were generally unable to fulfil their task as censors without excessive delays. New regulations were drawn up and issued in 1558: Now the deans of the University faculties constituted the censorship committee under the chairmanship of the rector. The printers' correctors had to promise under oath that they would henceforth inform the committee about dangerous books to be printed in their respective houses. But even this measure was only partly successful.

[28]Quoted by P. Burckhardt, "David Joris und seine Gemeinde in Basel," BZ 48 (1949), p. 42, Cf. *Opera Calvini*, vol. 16, 549 (July 28, 1557).

[29]Michel de Montaigne, "Journal de voyage en Italie," in: *Oeuvres complètes* (Bibliothèque de la Pléiade, Paris, 1962), pp. 1108, 1128ff.

[30]*Opera Calvini*, vol. 15, 209 (August 7, 1554). On the increasing alienation between Basel and Geneva cf. Uwe Plath, *Calvin und Basel in den Jahren 1552–1556* (Basel und Stuttgart, 1974), pp. 27f, 94ff, 173ff.

[31]StAB, Kirchenakten 9, 436f (September 11, 1563).

[32]Hans Berner, "Basel und das Zweite Helvetische Bekenntnis," in: *Zwingliana*, vol. 15 (1979/1), pp. 8–39.

[33]Basel's geographical situation between the Empire and the Swiss League created many conflicts and pressures throughout the 16th century. Sulzer's church policy is only one aspect of the problem. The very complicated and hitherto neglected topic has recently been treated in a comprehensive study, "Basels politisches Dilemma in der Reformationszeit," by the Basel historian Julia Gauss. This article will be published shortly in *Zwingliana*. I am grateful to Dr. Gauss for having permitted me to read her manuscript before publication.

[34]P. Burckhardt, *Geschichte der Stadt Basel*, p. 38ff; André Chèvre, *Jacques-Christophe de Wartensee, Prince-évêque de Bâle* (Delémont, 1963), pp. 253–277.

[35]M. Geiger, *Die Basler Kirche*, p. 28.

[36]*Ibid.*, p. 42ff.

[37]Ernst Staehelin, *Amandus Polanus von Polansdorf* (Basel, 1955), pp. 9–26.

[38]Frantisek Hrubý (ed.), *Etudiants tchèques aux écoles protestantes de l'Europe occidentale à la fin du 16e et au début du 17e siècle* (Brno, 1970). This volume contains many letters of Bohemians and Moravians to their Basel teachers and friends. Most of the originals are preserved in the Basel University Library, Ms. G II 12. For details see H.R. Guggisberg, "Das reformierte Basel als geistiger Brennpunkt Europas im 16. Jahrhundert," in: *Ecclesia semper reformanda*, p. 63ff.

[39]The hitherto published volumes of the *Amerbachkorrespondenz* (ed. by A. Hartmann and B.R. Jenny) contain the materials down to the year 1552 (vol. 8, Basel, 1974).

[40]StAB, Universitätsarchiv: Rationes rectoratus, 4 volumes: 1533–1569, 1569–1595, 1595–1627, 1592–1633 (K 8). The last two volumes are partly identical. There are also account books of the faculties of medicine, law, and philosophy as well as a "Liber legatorum." I am dealing here with the Rationes rectoratus exclusively. My investiga-

tions were greatly facilitated by the support and advice I received from Dr. Elisabeth Landolt. The early period of the financial history of the University has been studied by J. Rosen, "Die Universität Basel im Staatshaushalt 1460 bis 1535, in: BZ 72 (1972), pp. 137–219. Very important for the financial history of the University are also the weekly account books of the city government, the so-called "Wochenrechnungen."
[41]*Die Matrikel der Universität Basel*, vol. 2, p. 63; cf. Anne Jacobson Schutte, *Pier Paolo Vergerio: the Making of an Italian Reformer* (Geneva, 1976), p. 264, n. 37.
[42]Ed. by L. Haas in *Quellen zur Schweizergeschichte*, Abt. III, vol. 6 (Basel, 1956).
[43]Rationes rectoratus: 1556/57 (Vermigli), 1552/53 and 1554/55 (Gribaldi), 1553/54 (Lelio Sozzini).
[44]Rationes rectoratus: 1554/55.
[45]Rationes rectoratus: 1562/63, 1574/75, 1582/83, 1585/86.
[46]Rationes rectoratus: 1551/52. U. Plath, *Calvin und Basel*, p. 36f.
[47]Rationes rectoratus: 1551/52, 1552/53, 1559/60, 1569/70, 1581/82.
[48]Rationes rectoratus: 1556/57.
[49]Rationes rectoratus: 1578/79 (May 7, 1578). Cf. Donald R. Kelley, *François Hotman, a Revolutionary's Ordeal* (Princeton, N.J., 1973), p. 277.
[50]Rationes rectoratus: 1579/80, 1580/81, 1582/83, 1583/84. For Montaigne's visit cf. D.R. Kelley, *o.c.*, p. 285.
[51]Cf. Rationes rectoratus: 1549/50, 1551/52, 1554/55, 1565/66.
[52]Rationes rectoratus: 1579/80, 1580/81, 1581/82.
[53]Wurstisen was the author of the very valuable *Basler Chronik*, which was published in 1580 by Sebastian Henricpetri.

Chapter IV

[1]The title of Cherler's poem is *Epitaphium D. Sebastiani Castellionis*. It was republished twice in 1565: once in Cherler's *Luctus Ecclesiae et Academiae Basiliensis ob calamitatem recens acceptam* (a collection of poems written after the plague of 1563/64), a second time in a new edition of Castellio's *Dialogi sacri*. Both volumes came from the press of Oporinus. On Castellio's last illness and on the reactions caused at Zürich and Geneva by the news of his death, see H.R. Guggisberg, *Sebastian Castellio im Urteil seiner Nachwelt vom Späthumanismus bis zur Aufklärung* (Basel und Stuttgart, 1956), p. 11ff.
[2]*Ibid.*, p. 16.
[3]Ferdinand Buisson, *Sébastien Castellion, sa vie et son oeuvre* (Paris, 1892), vol. 2, p. 264f.
[4]The letter was published by F. Buisson, *o.c.*, vol. 2, p. 483ff. Bodenstein's accusations were based upon those contained in the preface of the French New Testament, edited by Calvin and Beza in 1559/60 and on Beza's *Responsio ad defensiones . . . S. Castellionis* (1563). Castellio's translation of Ochino's *Dialogi XXX* was published by Pietro Perna in 1563.
[5]Delio Cantimori, *Italienische Haeretiker der Spätrenaissance*, pp. 255, 461ff.
[6]F. Buisson, *o.c.*, vol. 2, p. 275ff.
[7]Cf. D. Cantimori, *o.c.*, p. 99ff; Werner Kaegi, *Humanistische Kontinuität im konfessionellen Zeitalter*, p. 10ff.
[8]The first edition of the *Dialogi sacri* appeared in October 1542 (Geneva: Jean Girard). It was to be revised and enlarged by the author on several occasions. In 1543 already, Castellio published *Dialogorum sacrorum liber secundus et tertius* (Geneva: Jean Girard). The first two Basel editions appeared in 1545. Cf. F. Buisson, *o.c.*, vol. 1, p. 152ff; vol. 2, p. 341f (Bibliography).
[9]*Opera Calvini*, vol. 11 (CR 39), 674–676.
[10]"Defensio ad authorem libri, cui titulus est, Calumniae Nebulonis," in: *Sebastiani*

Castelliones Dialogi IIII (Aresdorffij: per Theophilum Philadelphum [i.e. Basel: Pietro Perna], 1578), p. 10ff. The same tract—it was written in 1558—contains autobiographical information also on Castellio's father, of his studies at Lyon, and on his relationship with Calvin before 1544, pp. 14, 21f, 26f.

[11]Michel de Montaigne, *Essais* (Bibl. de la Pléiade, Paris, 1953), p. 261. Pierre Bayle, *Dictionnaire historique et critique* (2nd edition, Rotterdam, 1702), vol. 1, p. 837ff.

[12]Cf. the prefatory letter of Castellio's translation of the Book of Psalms: *Psalterium, reliquaque sacrarum literarum carmina* . . . (Basel: Oporinus, 1547).

[13]D. Cantimori, *o.c.*, p. 104f. Markus Kutter, *Celio Secondo Curione, sein Leben und Werk* (Basel, 1955).

[14]*Opera Calvini*, vol. 15 (CR 43), 19–22.

[15]*Ibid.*, vol. 8 (= CR 36), 453–644.

[16]*De haereticis, an sint persequendi, et omnino quomodo sit cum eis agendum* . . . (Magdeburgi, per Georgium Rausch, Anno Domini 1554. Mense Martio), cf. facsimile edition of Sape van der Woude (Geneva: Droz, 1954).

[17]*Traicté des hérétiques, a savoir si on les doit persécuter, et comment on se doit conduire avec eux* . . . (Rouen: Pierre Freneau, 1554). There is a modern edition of the French version of the *De Haereticis* by A. Olivet (Geneva, 1913). The supplementary texts are by C. Hedio, J. Agricola, J. Schenk, Chr. Hoffmann and from the Codex Justinianus. There has been a long debate on how and where the *Traicté des hérétiques* was published. Some years ago, the late Eugénie Droz has tried to show that the volume was printed in Lyon by Michel Châtillon, the brother of Sébastien, in 1557 or 1558. As editor and author of the prefatory letter she identified Jean Gète, minister at Bavans in the county of Montbéliard. Cf. "Castellioniana," in: E. Droz, *Chemins de l'hérésie*, vol. 2 (Geneva, 1971), pp. 325ff, 355ff. Convincing as these conclusions are, they do not rest upon definite evidence.

[18]*Correspondance de Théodore de Bèze*, recueillie par H. Aubert, publiée par F. Aubert et H. Meylan, vol. 1 (Geneva: Droz, 1960), p. 123 (March 29 [1554]).

[19]Cf. Roland H. Bainton's introduction to his English translation of the *De Haereticis: Concerning heretics, whether they are to be persecuted and how they are to be treated* . . . (New York: Columbia Univ. Press, 1935; repr. Octagon Books, 1965), p. 5ff; see also S. van der Woude's introduction to the facsimile edition, p. v ff. Eugénie Droz identified Georgius Kleinberg as David Joris, cf. "Castellioniana," p. 430. Another pseudonym which Castellio planned to use a few years later, was "Fridericus Rottenfelsius." It stands on the first page of the ms. copy of the *Dialogi IIII* which were to be published by Pietro Perna in 1578. In the printed book the name "Fridericus Rottenfelsius" does not appear, however. H.R. Guggisberg, "Pietro Perna," p. 185.

[20]S. van der Woude, *l.c.*, p.v; F. Buisson, *o.c.*, vol. 2, p. 2.

[21]The full title is *De Haereticis a civili magistratu puniendis libellus, adversus Martini Bellii farraginem et novorum Academicorum sectam*. The tract is often referred to as *Anti-Bellius*. In 1560 Nicolas Colladon published a French translation: *Traitté de l'autorité du magistrat*.

[22]This is particularly evident in Castellio's tracts which were published by Perna in 1578. A comparison of the ms. copy used by Perna with the printed texts shows that some of Castellio's sharpest counterattacks were omitted. Thus, the general tone of his argument appears less passionate than it was meant to appear. Cf. H.R. Guggisberg, "Pietro Perna," pp. 186–190.

[23]Cf. F. Buisson, *o.c.*, vol. 2, pp. 365, 372ff. Castellio also wrote a refutation of the *Anti-Bellius* of Théodore de Bèze. The title is *De haereticis a civili magistratu non puniendis, pro Martini Bellii farragine, adversus libellum Theodori Bezae libellus. Authore Basilio Montfortio*. This tract was edited by B. Becker and M. F. Valkhoff as volume 118 of the series *Travaux d'Humanisme et Renaissance* (Geneva, 1971).

[24]H.R. Guggisberg, "Pietro Perna," p. 191; A. Rotondò, "Pietro Perna," pp. 319–329; StAB, Handel und Gewerbe JJJ 6, foll. 48–51.

[25]F. Buisson, *o.c.*, vol. 2, p. 104ff.

[26]*Ibid.*, p. 133ff.

[27]For full bibliographical information see again F. Buisson, *o.c.*, vol. 2, p. 341ff. Additional materials are listed in our study on *Sebastian Castellio im Urteil seiner Nachwelt*, p. 177ff. The *Conseil à la France désolée* has been published in a modern edition with an introduction by Marius F. Valkhoff (Geneva, 1967).

[28]"De arte dubitandi et confidendi, ignorandi et sciendi," ed. Elisabeth Feist, in: *Reale Academia d'Italia, studi e documenti* 7 (Rome, 1937), pp. 277–430. The chapter "De justificatione" was published in Gouda, 1613. B. Becker, "Iets naar aanleiding van Castellio's Tractatus de justificatione," *Nederlands Archief voor Kerkgeschiedinis* #39 (1952), pp. 124–132. A new and complete edition of *De arte dubitandi* was published by Elisabeth Feist Hirsch in 1981 (Leiden: E.J. Brill).

[29]"Sebastianus Castalio Eduardo Sexto Angliae Regi clariss. Salutem," *Biblia, interprete Sebastiano Castalione, una cum eiusdem annotationibus* (Basel: Oporinus, 1551)., foll. 2ro - 5ro. A close examination of the first paragraph reveals that Castellio dedicated his Latin Bible to the youthful king because he wanted to make his name known in England. Thus he alludes to the fact that a Latin translation, undertaken at the king's order, has been left unfinished because one of the two translators died. Without mentioning any names, Castellio obviously refers to the enterprise of Martin Bucer and Paul Fagius. Fagius had died on November 23, 1549. Now Castellio offers his own work to fill the gap. The same paragraph contains indirect compliments to Sir John Cheke, the "magister eruditus" of the young king, and Castellio also mentions the fact that England has become a haven of peace for continental refugees. This seems to show that the Savoyard humanist contemplated a move to England at the time when he suffered excessive poverty in Basel. He obviously hoped for a remuneration or even for an invitation to one of the universities. His hopes were not to be fulfilled, however. Cf. H.R. Guggisberg, "Sebastian Castellio und die englische Reformation," in: *Festgabe Hans von Greyerz* (Bern, 1967), pp. 319–338.

[30]In 1557 and 1563 respectively. Both works were published by Oporinus.

[31]*De haereticis* (ed. S. van der Woude), pp. 118–124.

[32]*Ibid.*, p. 122f.

[33]*Ibid.*, p. 13: "Primum [periculum], ne quis pro haeretico habeatur, qui non sit haereticus . . . Alterum periculum est, ne si quis vere sit haereticus, is gravius, aut aliter puniatur, quam postulet Christiana disciplina."

[34]*Ibid.*, pp. 12ff, 22f.

[35]*Contra libellum Calvini* (1612), art. 77: "Hominem occidere, non est doctrinam tueri, sed est hominem occidere."

[36]*De haereticis*, p. 20, also p. 125ff ("Quantum orbi noceant persecutiones, sententia Georgii Kleinbergi"). See also *Contra libellum Calvini*, fol. lvii ro ff. Cf. Marcelle Derwa, "L'influence de l'esprit irénique sur le contenu doctrinal de la pensée de Castellion," in: *Revue belge de philologie et d'histoire* 58 (1980), pp. 355–381. Based mainly on *De arte dubitandi*, this perceptive study stresses not only the simplicity and straightforwardness, but also the inexorability and logical coherence of Castellio's argument.

[37]H.R. Guggisberg, *Sebastian Castellio im Urteil seiner Nachwelt*, p. 145ff.

[38]*De haereticis*, p. 74ff.

[39]*Ibid.*, p. 109f; cf. R.H. Bainton, *Concerning Heretics*, p. 204, n.1.

[40]R.H. Bainton, Introduction to *Concerning Heretics*, p. 93ff.

[41]Friedrich Heer, in *Die dritte Kraft* (Frankfurt a.M., 1959), pp. 279, 282, 701 repeatedly stresses the influence of Nicholas of Cusa on Castellio.

[42]*De arte dubitandi*, ed. E. F. Hirsch (Leiden, 1981) n. 85 p. 383ff. Cf. Johannes Kühn, *Toleranz und Offenbarung* (Leipzig, 1923), p. 328.

[43]*De arte dubitandi*, p. 314; cf. *De justificatione* (Gouda, 1613), p. 3ff.

[44]H.R. Guggisberg, "Castellio und der Ausbruch der Religionskriege in Frankreich," in: ARG (1977), pp. 253–266, esp. 264f. Cf. also P.G. Bietenholz, *Basle and France*, pp. 122ff, 218ff. The *Exhortation aux princes* is now generally attributed to Etienne Pasquier.

[45]H.R. Guggisberg, "Sebastian Castellio on the Power of the Christian Prince," in: L. Krieger, F. Stern (eds.), *The Responsibility of Power, Historical Essays in honor of Hajo Holborn* (Garden City, N.Y., 1967), pp. 64–84.

[46]For more detailed information cf. our study on *Sebastian Castellio im Urteil seiner Nachwelt*, pp. 48ff, 68ff.

[47]Sozzini had met Castellio personally on a visit to Basel in 1563. He alludes to this fact in his *Defensio disputationis suae de loco septimi capitis Epistolae ad Romanos* (1595). Cf. *Bibliotheca Fratrum Polonorum* (Irenopoli = [Amsterdam], 1656), vol. 1, p. 126, col. 2.

[48]Lech Szczucki, "Polski przektad dialogu Castelliona," *Archiwum Historii Filozofii i Mysli Spolecznej* 9 (1963), pp. 143–168.

[49]Antal Pirnàt, "Jacobus Paleologus," *Studia nad Arianizmem*, ed. L. Chmaj (Warsaw, 1959), pp. 73–129.

[50]H.R. Guggisberg, *Sebastian Castellio im Urteil seiner Nachwelt*, p. 105ff.

[51]*Ibid.*, p. 109; cf. H.R. Guggisberg, "Religious Freedom and the History of the Chistian World in Roger Williams' Thought," in: *Early American Literature* 12 (1977), pp. 36–48, esp. p. 44.

[52]The most important among them is Ferdinand Buisson (1841–1932). He was general inspector and subsequently director of primary education in France. In 1896 he became professor of education at the Sorbonne. As a member of the radical-socialist party he was a deputy in the French parliament from 1902 to 1924. Buisson was a founder and president of the League of Human Rights and received the Peace Nobel Prize in 1927. His interest in Castellio was based upon the ideas of the movement of "Christianisme libéral." Buisson started his research in 1867 while he was a professor at the Academy (later University) of Neuchâtel (Switzerland). In 1891 he submitted his work to the Sorbonne as a "Thèse de doctorat." Cf. *Historisch-Biographisches Lexikon der Schweiz*, vol. 2, p. 422.

[53]We think particularly of Earl Morse Wilbur and Roland H. Bainton. Wilbur has written the standard *History of Unitarianism* (2 vols., Cambridge, Mass., 1946, 1952), while Bainton, in addition to his English translation of Castellio's *De haereticis*, has produced a large number of important studies on the "champion of religious liberty." Some of these studies are included in Bainton's *Studies on the Reformation* (London, 1963).

Index of Names